A Teacher's Guide to VITAL Collaboration

Facilitating Evidence-Driven Inquiry in PLCs to Improve Teaching and Learning

Kevin Perks

TEACHERS COLLEGE PRESS
TEACHERS COLLEGE | COLUMBIA UNIVERSITY
NEW YORK AND LONDON

WestEd
WestEd.org

Published by Teachers College Press,® 1234 Amsterdam Avenue, New York, NY 10027, and WestEd, 730 Harrison Street, San Francisco, CA 94107

Front cover photos by (clockwise from top): Goodboy Picture Company; SDI Productions; and SolStock, all via iStock by Getty Images.

Library of Congress Cataloging-in-Publication Data is available at loc.gov

ISBN 978-0-8077-8702-1 (paper)
ISBN 978-0-8077-8703-8 (hardcover)
ISBN 978-0-8077-8304-7 (ebook)

Printed on acid-free paper
Manufactured in the United States of America

Praise for *A Teacher's Guide to VITAL Collaboration*

"Kevin Perks' companion books—one for school leaders, the other for teachers—contain magnificent, powerful, and clear ideas for transforming learning in schools. The fourfold framework is comprehensive and instantly inspiring. In our current work on deep change, we look for 'specificity without imposition,' 'proximity to practice,' 'leader-teacher-student collaboration,' and clear, measurable outcomes. These two books have it all: a clear pathway for principals, teachers, and students to work together and get results. Readers will benefit immeasurably by immersing their work in these inspiring companion books. VITAL Collaboration, indeed!"

—**Michael Fullan**, professor emeritus, University of Toronto, and author of *The New Meaning of Educational Change,* Sixth Edition

"This practical, accessibly written guidebook provides faculty with a process for working together to create a culture in which inquiry and growth are promoted among both teachers and students. In a profession where many feel isolated, this book's road-tested procedures can help teachers develop ways of working together to address the issues they face in their classrooms and schools."

—**Peter Smagorinsky**, emeritus professor, The University of Georgia

"*A Teacher's Guide to VITAL Collaboration* provides educators with protocols to support their PLC practices, allowing teams to make meaningful improvements in student outcomes and overall increase collective teacher efficacy. Recognizing the complexity of teaching and learning, the VITAL collaboration process offers the roadmap to shared growth!"

—**Jennifer Loftus**, superintendent, Paso Robles Joint Unified School District, former executive director of educational services, Santa Maria-Bonita School District

"This terrific resource describes and synergizes collaboration among professionals within school structures and teams to maximize solutions. The practical approaches, resources, and tools are useful for impactful collaboration within our school teams."

—**Mary E. Little**, professor and program coordinator, Exceptional Student Education, University of Central Florida

"This book offers a transformative approach to Professional Learning Communities (PLCs) through the VITAL Collaboration model. By using concrete evidence from teacher practice and student learning, it provides clear strategies for fostering both teacher and student growth. With practical tools and research-backed insights, this guide helps educators and leaders maximize the impact of every PLC session. A valuable resource for anyone committed to continuous improvement in education, specifically scholarly practitioner researchers."

—**Juliann Sergi McBrayer**, codirector, National Youth Advocacy and Resilience Research Center, and associate professor, educational leadership, Georgia Southern University

Contents

Acknowledgments

Reflecting on all who have supported me in this endeavor of writing this book and its companion, *A School Leader's Guide to VITAL Collaboration*, is profoundly humbling. I am reminded of the apple trees outside my window. As an amateur orchardist, I've come to appreciate the beauty and resilience of these trees. Though we often focus on the fruit hanging from the branches, the real magic happens out of sight, in the root system underground. The microscopic fibers at the ends of the roots draw essential nutrients from the earth, while the deep roots, often as extensive as the tree is tall, provide strength and stability. The support system that has bolstered me to complete this book is equally deep and steadfast.

First, I must thank my family: my wife Jessica, my daughter Celia, and my parents. Your unwavering support is a daily blessing. Jessica, you are my sun. Celia, you are the air I breathe. Mom and Dad, you are the ground beneath my feet. I would be remiss to overlook Reeses and Millie as well. Reeses, ever loyal, more faithful than a shadow. And Millie, a gentle reminder to get outside and take a walk.

Next, to my work family. At the top of this family tree are Johanna Barmore and Melissa Strand, whose vision, dedication, and tireless efforts have been instrumental in nurturing VITAL from a wild seedling into a mature service that is transforming schools. Johanna and Melissa, your ability to bring clarity and structure to my often-scattered ideas is nothing short of extraordinary. Your insight, patience, and unwavering commitment to excellence have left an indelible mark on this book. Truly, your fingerprints are on every page, and I am endlessly grateful for your partnership in this journey.

My gratitude also extends to the Quality Schools and Districts team, who have continually improved VITAL through their dedication to supporting schools nationwide. This includes Bejanae, Cerelle, Erica, Faith, Jason, Kailey, Krystal, Roxanne, Susan, Tammy, and Tom. I'm also deeply grateful to Leslie and Ursula for their constant encouragement and support, as well as Bob, Maria, Sofia, and Terry, who push me to be better every day. As Terry often reminds me, "All things are VITAL." Last, but not least, my thanks to Robin, who provided excellent feedback on both drafts and has been a constant support.

I must also thank my Noble and UNH families from years past: Heidi, Kate, and Rick. You were the first to show me the power of a true professional learning community. You made me a better teacher every day. This book is a small attempt to capture and share that magic. Mike, you have been a colleague, thought partner and friend since the beginning of my career. Thanks for being a constant inspiration.

Of course, my thanks to my editor, Allison, who has helped make all this possible. I cannot thank you enough.

Lastly, to all the teachers working tirelessly and often without recognition, who strive every day to support our students, our future. This book would be meaningless without you.

CHAPTER 1

An Introduction to VITAL Collaboration

PRE-READING PROMPTS

- Why did you open this book? What are you hoping to learn or get out of it? What questions do you hope it answers?
- What experiences have you had collaborating with others as an educator? When have these experiences excelled? Why did these stand out?
- Do you think teachers have enough opportunities to collaborate? Why or why not?
- Why do you think it is important for teachers to collaborate routinely?

INTRODUCTION

Welcome to *A Teacher's Guide to VITAL Collaboration*. You might have opened this book because you are interested in learning more about teacher collaboration in schools. Perhaps you are part of a professional learning community (PLC) and are looking for ways to strengthen it or make it even more productive. Maybe you are a PLC facilitator wanting to hone your facilitation skills. Or you might be a school leader seeking to understand what effective collaboration in PLCs looks like, so you can better support your teachers. Whatever your reason, we thank you for joining us on this journey.

In this book, you will learn how to create and sustain high-impact collaborative practices that directly enhance both teaching quality and student achievement. Whether you're a teacher, facilitator, or school leader, this guide provides actionable tools and insights to transform collaboration in your school. We hope it becomes a valued resource that helps you in your personal and professional learning journey.

Before diving into the content, I want to share two personal experiences I had as an educator. Before I do, I encourage you to take a moment to reflect. Close your eyes and think about a time when you had a positive experience collaborating with others. Re-immerse yourself in that moment. What did you see and hear? What else did you notice? How did you feel, and why? Take a few moments to reflect before reading on. Once you've reflected, consider how your experiences compare to the ones I share below.

Experience 1—My First Experience of Formal Teaching

It was my first day of real teaching. I can still see the sun streaming in through the tall, narrow windows of the urban middle school classroom in Chicago. I was barely in my 20s, wearing ironed khakis and the tie my girlfriend bought me as a gift. I sat with three of my colleagues in the hushed early hours, in chairs too small for us, surrounded by scattered papers and notes. Together, we were building a lesson, refining each idea as we imagined how students might react, where they might stumble, and where they might excel.

A bit later, I stood in front of a class of 6th-graders, while the rest of my team settled around the room with notebooks in hand, capturing everything—the way a student's hand shot up, a quiet nod of understanding, shared laughter, and furrowed brows of frustration. As I taught, their pencils raced, recording not only what we said as teachers but also what students said and how their eyes lit up or flickered with hesitation.

In the afternoon, we gathered again, stacks of student work between us, voices rising and falling as we shared our observations. What had sparked students' engagement? Where had confusion crept in? Who needed extra support? By the time we looked up, late afternoon shadows were falling, and the hallways were silent. We stayed, diving back into planning, building the next day's lesson based on what we had learned. We repeated this rhythm for weeks, each cycle revealing something new about our students, our teaching, and ourselves. It was a blast.

Experience 2—My First Inservice PLC

The first time I joined a true professional learning community as an inservice teacher, I had recently moved to a rural high school in the Northeast. I had been teaching for many years at this point. It was the first week of school, and the windows revealed trees in the early stages of changing color. Our days followed a 2-day block schedule, with 80-minute classes that allowed lessons to breathe. Every other day, one of those blocks was dedicated to our 10th-grade team's PLC.

During our first PLC meeting, I sat at a long, scarred table in our team's shared workspace. Rick, the math teacher, sat to my left; Heidi, the science teacher, was across from me; and Kate, the social studies teacher, was on my right. As the new English teacher, I listened as they shared their hopes for our students and our plans for the year. There was a strong sense of purpose in the room, an openness that reminded me of my preservice days. As a team we were collectively responsible for the success of our students.

We began by sharing our initial plans for instruction. There was an excitement as we turned ideas into something cohesive, each suggestion sparking new insights. Later, we would step into each other's classrooms to see firsthand how our plans were coming alive. During one observation, I noticed how Rick taught a math concept with such clarity that the students' heads nodded in unison. I scribbled notes, wondering how I could adapt his approach to my English class.

Often, after observing each other, we gathered in our next PLC meeting to trade notes and stories—the expressions we'd seen on students' faces, the moments they leaned in, or times their eyes glazed over. We laughed, puzzled over solutions, and dug through student work together, searching for clues of understanding or signs that something wasn't connecting. Each session felt like piecing together a map to guide our teaching.

Looking back, I realize how rare that kind of collaboration was. We weren't just teaching; we were honing our craft for our students. We set goals, buckled down and made adjustments when something didn't work, and celebrated the small victories in our students' progress. Those years with my team provided some of the most fulfilling and transformative experiences of my career.

REFLECTING ON OUR EXPERIENCES

How did my experiences compare with yours? They were likely different in many ways, but perhaps similar in others. I share these memories to emphasize something I've learned in my 30 years as an educator—a lesson firmly supported by research: We are often at our best when working and collaborating with like-minded colleagues, especially when we are trying to improve. These early experiences taught me that collaboration is most powerful when it is structured, intentional, and focused on shared growth. In addition, when collaboration is at its best it brings energy, joy, and growth. Steven Johnson (2010), in his book *Where Good Ideas Come From: The Natural History of Innovation*, reminds us that our ideas often need the insights and experiences of others to reach their fullest potential. It is my hope that this book helps you and those you work with optimize your own ideas, ensuring they have a powerful impact on the students you serve.

WHO WE ARE

We are part of the Quality Schools and Districts team at WestEd. WestEd is a nonprofit, nonpartisan, research, development, and service agency that has worked with education communities across the country for over 50 years to promote excellence, achieve equity, and improve learning for all children, youth, and adults, particularly those historically underserved. Our staff provides a broad range of services focused on generating knowledge and applying evidence to help educators and leaders improve policies, systems, and practices. As school improvement specialists, my group provides professional learning and technical assistance to support school improvement efforts nationwide.

WHAT DO WE DO?

A core focus of our work on the Quality Schools and Districts team is supporting instructional transformation at the school level. Much of our work involves direct training and professional development around evidence-based practices. This includes building schools' capacity to help teachers apply what they learn during professional development.

Many of the schools we work with struggle to structure time for teachers to collaborate and enhance their instructional practice. To strengthen their capacity to implement and sustain robust collaboration, we have developed a powerful framework over the past 10 years: VITAL Collaboration. This is a shortform for *Visibly Improving Teaching and Learning through Collaboration*. We have used VITAL to help numerous schools improve, including many Comprehensive Support and Improvement (CSI) schools, which are among the lowest performing in their state or have the lowest graduation rates. VITAL has helped many of these schools move out of this status.

PURPOSE

This book aims to share the VITAL Collaboration framework we have developed over a decade of helping schools transform their instructional practices. The challenges facing educators today are urgent, and collaboration is a part of the solution that can no longer be postponed. By diving into this book, you'll find tools to make collaboration an integral part of your professional practice. We have found that routine collaboration focused on improving instruction is an essential component of school improvement. However, we frequently visit schools that have few or no collaborative structures. We use the term "collaborative structure" deliberately, recognizing that there are various ways teachers can work in teams, such as critical friends groups, data teams, student achievement teams, and professional learning communities, to name a few. For simplicity, we primarily use the terms "Professional Learning Communities (PLCs)" and "teacher teams" throughout this book to refer to any group of teachers that meets regularly to enhance their professional practice and improve student outcomes.

WHO THIS BOOK IS FOR

As the title suggests, this book is written for teachers interested in building their capacity to lead or participate in collaborative efforts, such as PLCs. Readers will gain a deeper understanding of the importance of collective teacher efficacy and how collaborative structures like PLCs can improve teaching quality. You will be introduced to a collection of helpful protocols designed to facilitate conversations dedicated to improving teaching practice. Readers will also deepen their knowledge of how to foster and sustain the types of collaboration that can transform instruction and improve student achievement.

Transformative school leaders will also find this book invaluable as a companion to *A School Leader's Guide to VITAL Collaboration*. While the *School Leader's Guide* focuses on the leadership practices essential for implementing VITAL Collaboration, this book dives deeper into the architecture of VITAL Collaboration—the practices and strategies teachers and PLC facilitators need to employ within PLCs to improve teaching and learning.

What If Our School Already Has PLCs?

If your school already has PLCs or similar approaches to teacher meetings, such as data teams or achievement teams, this book will still be valuable. Part II of this book provides guidance on how to be an effective facilitator regardless of the collaborative model your school uses. The protocols in Part III are designed as resources for facilitators to guide their teams through the four phases of the VITAL framework, but these protocols can also be used as stand-alone resources within any approach to PLCs. We encourage readers to use these resources to bolster collaboration however it is conceived and structured in their school.

What If We Do Not Have PLCs?

If your school has not yet established any form of PLC, this book offers a roadmap to build them from the ground up. The process begins with understanding the foundational principles of collaboration and then moves into creating the structures and routines necessary for PLCs to flourish. VITAL Collaboration provides step-by-step guidance on setting up PLCs that align with school goals, focus on feedback, and are grounded in standards. Whether starting from scratch or refining existing practices, *The Teacher's Guide to VITAL Collaboration* will serve as a roadmap for creating PLCs that make a real difference.

HOW THIS BOOK IS ORGANIZED

The book is divided into four sections. Part I introduces VITAL Collaboration and includes two chapters beyond this one. The next chapter makes the case for VITAL Collaboration by reviewing research that shows the importance of and a pathway for collaboration that can strengthen collective teacher efficacy. Chapter 3 provides an overview of the four phases of VITAL Collaboration, key principles, and a description of the roles and responsibilities of teachers, facilitators, and school leaders.

Part II of this book contains three chapters designed to boost the facilitation skills of teachers who lead PLCs or team meetings. Chapter 4 describes the essential characteristics of an effective facilitator. Chapter 5 explores key practices and strategies for effective facilitation. Chapter 6 addresses common challenges facilitators face in PLCs and provides guidance for navigating them.

Part III provides what we consider to be an essential toolbox for PLC facilitators. Chapter 7 introduces these elements, and Chapters 8 through 16 provide core protocols for implementing all four phases of the VITAL Collaboration framework, including protocols for getting started, engaging in teaching and learning cycles, and monitoring progress and celebrating success. The final part of the book, Part IV, offers additional tools and ideas that provide additional knowledge for guiding PLCs. Each chapter can stand alone but also complements topics introduced earlier.

SUGGESTIONS FOR USING THIS BOOK

Readers can engage with the content of this book in several ways. While we believe any educator can pick up this book, read it cover to cover, and find it useful, it may not come as a surprise that we recommend a more collaborative approach. First, we encourage readers to engage with the content in a collaborative setting. For example, we recommend that PLCs read this book, or sections of it, together. To encourage reflection and discussion, most chapters include pre-reading prompts at the beginning and prompts for further reflection and discussion at the end. These are designed to prepare readers to engage in upcoming content and to process what they recently learned. Some chapters also include case studies at the elementary, middle, and high school levels to illustrate some of the concepts introduced in a chapter and to serve as springboards to promote additional inquiry and discussion.

Lastly, you can access the resources and protocols in this book through the QR code on the following page. Scanning the code will direct you to a landing page where you can find and download the latest versions of the tools and resources in this book.

CONCLUSION

Collaboration is more than an occasional meeting with colleagues; it is a driving force behind continuous improvement in teaching and student learning. It is often the difference between schools that improve and those that don't. However, fostering effective collaboration requires more than simply setting aside time to meet—it calls for intentionality, structure, and skilled facilitation.

In the following pages, we introduce VITAL Collaboration—our research-based and field-tested approach to help educators engage in meaningful collaboration. In Chapter 2, we will delve deeper into the research that informs this kind of collaboration. In Chapter 3, we introduce and walk through all four phases of the framework. This framework centers on visibly improving teaching and learning through cycles of inquiry, data-driven discussions, and collective goal-setting. As you prepare to explore VITAL Collaboration, consider how this approach might address the challenges and aspirations you've experienced, and how it can transform your PLCs into engines of schoolwide improvement.

PROMPTS FOR REFLECTION AND DISCUSSION

- After reading this Introduction, what resonates with you the most? Why?
- Were any initial questions answered? If so, which ones?
- What questions are you left with?
- What are you looking forward to as you continue reading?

Part I

THE BASICS OF VITAL COLLABORATION

Part I of this book outlines the basics of VITAL Collaboration, offering readers a foundational understanding of its significance in improving teaching and learning through systematic, intentional collaboration. Chapter 2, "A Rationale for Collaborative Excellence," provides research-based insights into why collaboration is a critical driver of effective professional practice and educational improvement. It explores the challenges of sustaining collaborative work in schools and highlights research areas like collective teacher efficacy, improvement science, and professional learning communities that serve as pillars for the VITAL approach.

Chapter 3, "The Architecture of VITAL Collaboration: A Framework for Success," outlines the structure and phases of the VITAL Collaboration process. Here, readers will learn about the distinct components that guide teacher teams through a continuous improvement cycle, focused on enhancing instructional practice at the lesson level. This chapter also presents the roles and responsibilities that are essential for VITAL Collaboration to thrive, setting the stage for subsequent parts of the book that delve deeper into facilitation skills and collaborative protocols.

CHAPTER 2

A Rationale for Collaborative Excellence

PRE-READING PROMPTS

- Why is it important for teachers to collaborate?
- What is your understanding of the concept of collective teacher efficacy? How would you define it? Why do you think it is important?
- How familiar are you with the research behind improvement science, high-quality professional learning, PLCs, and lesson study? What might link these all together?
- What is the relationship between feedback and improvement? Why is feedback so important to improve teaching and learning?
- How often do teachers you work with receive helpful feedback that improves their teaching?
- How would you explain to someone else how school improvement works?

INTRODUCTION

Why should teachers collaborate? This is a question I sometimes pose to educators at workshops. Typically, I receive responses like, "Because it helps us learn" or "Because it helps us solve problems" or "More heads are better than one." I love these answers, but I like to dig deeper by asking, "As professionals, why do we want to learn more?" or "What kinds of problems are we trying to solve?"

These questions usually lead to answers like, "To get better at teaching." Great, but I push further: "Why do we want to get better at teaching?" The reply often comes, "Because it will help students learn and achieve more." Wonderful—but why do we want students to learn more? Ultimately, I hear answers like, "Because it's our job!" or "Because we want our students to reach their fullest potential." Exactly.

None of this is groundbreaking, but I believe it's crucial to connect the dots. In essence, as educators, we value collaboration because it has the potential to improve student outcomes. However, the journey from knowing that collaboration can enhance student outcomes to making it routine is not a simple one. This is something we see repeatedly in schools and districts across the country. Many schools struggle to create, implement, and sustain systems of collaboration that truly make a difference for teachers and students.

There are understandable reasons that many schools struggle to develop and sustain systems of collaboration that routinely improve teaching and learning. Two common explanations are competing priorities and a lack of resources. Regarding the first reason, schools today are responsible for so much that it can feel impossible to fit routine collaboration into the school day. When I ask school leaders to tell me what they are responsible for, they often mention a list of priorities: academic instruction, social–emotional learning, equity and inclusion, cultural responsiveness, career and college readiness, mental health support, digital and financial literacy, family and community engagement, health and nutrition, and more. Given all of this, it is no surprise school leaders find it difficult to fit collaboration into school schedules. In addition to competing priorities, schools also often face a lack of resources—from finding enough time during the school day to having the physical space for teachers to meet to ensuring enough staff are available to cover classes while educators collaborate.

Despite our belief that educators intuitively understand the importance of collaboration, the reality of life in schools—with all the competing priorities and myriad challenges—makes routine collaboration feel like a luxury that many schools simply cannot afford. Societal pressure can exacerbate this perception. Years ago, I served as a school board member, and every time the topic of PLCs came up, community members or other board members would comment that any time teachers were not working directly with students was time wasted. Many people believe the myth that once teachers graduate from college, they are fully trained and have all the skills they need. Every educator knows this is false and that teaching is challenging. Staying at the top of our game requires ongoing professional learning, reflection, and collaboration to continuously hone our craft.

MAKING A CASE FOR COLLABORATION

Given the challenges schools face in developing impactful systems of collaboration, it becomes essential to make the case for building such a system—one designed to improve teaching and learning. Below, we briefly review key research areas that inform our approach: collective teacher efficacy, improvement science, high-quality professional development, professional learning communities, and lesson study. Each of these areas provides essential insights into how collaboration can be structured to maximize its impact and why it is so important. They also set the stage for a Theory of Improvement we will share later as well.

Collective Teacher Efficacy

For a school to truly excel, it must cultivate a powerful sense of collective teacher efficacy. But what exactly does that mean? Imagine a school where every teacher believes not only in their own abilities but also in the collective strength of the entire teaching staff—a place where educators are united in their conviction and commitment that together they can overcome challenges and create exceptional learning experiences for all students. This concept is rooted in Bandura's (1977) work on self-efficacy, which he defined as the belief "in one's capacity to organize and execute the courses of action required to produce given attainments" (p. 3). The idea of self-efficacy can be expanded to collective teacher efficacy: the collective belief of a group of teachers in their ability to positively impact student achievement and overcome challenges. When a school achieves high levels of collective efficacy, its teachers are more likely to work together to provide consistent, high-quality instruction and unwavering support for all students (Hattie, 2023). It is the type of school every parent hopes for—a community where educators are empowered, collaborative, and deeply committed to ensuring every child succeeds.

The benefits of collective teacher efficacy are substantial, with research indicating a strong positive impact on both student achievement and school culture. In fact, Donohoo, Hattie, and Eells (2018) highlight that collective teacher efficacy is one of the most significant predictors of student success. It is even more predictive of student achievement than socioeconomic factors, home environment, or prior academic performance. In short, when educators believe in their collective ability to influence student outcomes, they are more likely to set challenging goals, engage in effective teaching practices, and demonstrate persistence in the face of challenges.

Further evidence supporting the importance of collective teacher efficacy comes from Goddard and colleagues (2004, 2017). They found that collective efficacy beliefs are not just an aggregate of individual self-efficacy beliefs but rather a unique group-level construct. Schools with high levels of collective efficacy show greater teacher collaboration, better student outcomes, and a culture of mutual support among teachers. In low-performing schools, enhancing collective efficacy has been linked to better academic performance and a stronger work ethic among teachers. Teachers in these schools are more likely to persist in their efforts, even when faced with challenges, because they view obstacles as temporary setbacks rather than insurmountable barriers (Mosoge et al., 2018).

In sum, the transformative power of collective teacher efficacy has been well established in research as a key factor for driving school improvement through high-quality teaching and learning. Schools that cultivate a strong sense of collective efficacy among their staff are more likely to see enhanced student learning outcomes, a collaborative school culture, and a resilient approach to overcoming challenges. As a result, investing in practices and leadership that support the development of collective efficacy is a critical strategy for achieving high-quality teaching and learning at the school level. This then begs the question: What can schools do to increase the collective efficacy of teaching? One body of research that provides an answer to this is improvement science.

Improvement Science

Improvement science is a structured process that can help teachers achieve sustainable improvements in their instruction by routinely exploring challenges, identifying potential strategies for improvement, testing them out and getting feedback, and finally analyzing the results. As such, it is an excellent approach to strengthening collective teacher efficacy. Central to its approach is the Plan-Do-Study-Act (PDSA) cycle (see Figure 2.1), which is an iterative process for conducting rapid cycles of inquiry and feedback that allow educators to make incremental changes to their practice (Lewis, 2015). The *Plan* phase involves identifying a problem, setting goals, and determining strategies for improvement. During the *Do* phase, teachers try out new techniques and receive feedback. During the *Study* phase, data are collected and analyzed to assess progress. Finally, in the *Act* phase, teachers determine and share what was learned and make decisions about next steps. This iterative cycle helps ensure that educators continuously learn from their collaborative experiences, refine their practices, and build a deeper understanding of what works best for their students.

The process of improvement science can also be amplified through the work of networked improvement communities (NICs), which bring together educators and teams working collaboratively toward a common goal (LeMahieu et al., 2017). Communities like this provide a structure for educators to engage in a shared process of inquiry across teams and individuals to collectively share and build knowledge about what works in their context to enhance teaching. This collaborative aspect of improvement science emphasizes that improvement is not a solitary endeavor but one that benefits from the collective wisdom of multiple voices (Bryk et al., 2011).

In addition to the PDSA cycle and NICs, there are other ideas drawn from improvement science that are particularly well-suited for strengthening collective teacher efficacy. One key is improvement science's focus on being problem-specific and teacher-centered. An improvement science approach begins by identifying specific problems of practice that teachers regularly wrestle with. This user-centered focus helps ensure that improvements

Figure 2.1. PDS Cycle

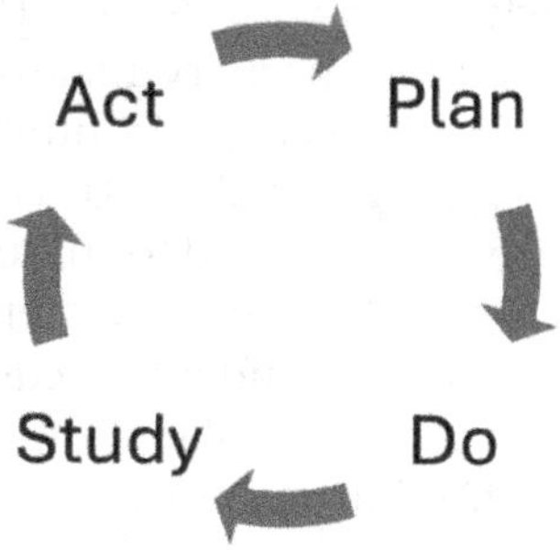

are relevant to the needs of both teachers and students (LeMahieu et al., 2015). Another important facet of improvement science is the use of routine feedback loops to help educators learn from their inquiries and trials of new ideas. Feedback loops, when guided by a PDSA cycle, allow teachers to apply new techniques, gather data, and make adjustments that foster a culture of continuous learning and adaptation (Lewis, 2015).

In sum, improvement science describes a powerful mechanism for building collective teacher efficacy. By engaging teachers in a shared process of problem-solving, testing, and refining instructional strategies, improvement science not only helps improve teaching practices but also strengthens teachers' belief in their collective ability to influence student success. For schools aiming to develop a culture of continuous improvement, integrating the principles of improvement science provides a pathway for empowering teachers, enhancing their practices, and ultimately improving student outcomes. This leads us to professional learning, which we believe is essential for effectively implementing an improvement science approach. We focus on two aspects of professional learning below: high-quality professional development and professional learning communities.

High-Quality Professional Development

Going a little further, we believe an improvement science approach to enhancing collective teacher efficacy can be optimized when it is connected to high-quality professional development (PD). Improvement science emphasizes the importance of having teachers try new strategies, test them out, and get feedback. This suggests the following questions: What are the best strategies to test out? How can we learn about them? The best answers vary by context. It is essential for teachers to have opportunities to engage in high-quality PD that introduces them to evidence-based practices as part of an overall continuous improvement process. Let's explore this a little more.

Effective PD centers on providing teachers with structured learning experiences that enhance teaching practice. Such PD is recognized as essential for teachers' ongoing growth and a primary means to support student learning in increasingly complex educational environments (Collin & Smith, 2021; Darling-Hammond et al., 2017). High-quality PD is crucial, as it directly impacts classroom practices, which are closely linked to student learning gains. Research underscores that well-structured PD equips teachers with the knowledge and skills necessary to address evolving student needs, especially in developing critical thinking, problem-solving, and collaboration skills (Darling-Hammond et al., 2017; Popova et al., 2022). Furthermore, effective PD contributes to narrowing achievement gaps, enhancing equity across diverse learning environments (Popova et al., 2022; Sims & Fletcher-Wood, 2021).

For PD to be effective, it should incorporate several key characteristic. Notably, high-quality PD should be content-focused, active, collaborative, and sustained (Darling-Hammond et al., 2017; Desimone & Garet, 2015). For example, to be effective PD should emphasize specific content knowledge, tailored to subject areas, that supports teachers in mastering the material they teach. This element allows for practical applications in classrooms, promoting subject-specific pedagogical techniques that can enhance student understanding (Darling-Hammond et al., 2017; Popova et al., 2022).

A few more characteristics are worth noting here. First, engaging teachers in the same types of activities they will use in their classrooms, such as analyzing student work or trying out teaching strategies, helps them transfer learning directly to their practices (Collin & Smith, 2021; Kennedy, 2016). Also, PD that leverages collaboration has shown efficacy in establishing long-lasting instructional improvements by embedding shared learning into school culture (Darling-Hammond et al., 2017; Desimone & Garet, 2015). Relatedly, sustaining PD over time allows teachers to reflect, implement new strategies, and refine their practices with ongoing feedback. Research suggests that programs lasting over an extended period with frequent engagement (e.g., 20+ hours) produce better outcomes compared to one-off sessions (Desimone & Garet, 2015; Popova et al., 2022). Finally, as emphasized in the improvement science research, building in time for reflection and feedback enables teachers to thoughtfully integrate PD insights into their teaching. Reflective practice solidifies learning and encourages the continuous refinement of instructional methods (Darling-Hammond et al., 2017; Sims & Fletcher-Wood, 2021).

Professional Learning Communities (PLCs)

Building on the research above, professional learning communities are an excellent vehicle through which to sustain PD and implement improvement science techniques. Most educators we work with are familiar with some form of PLC. As mentioned earlier in this book, we define PLCs generally as teams of teachers who meet and collaborate regularly to improve their teaching practices to enhance student outcomes. Traditional PLCs emphasize shared goals, mutual support, and ongoing professional growth through collective reflection and inquiry (Moosa et al., 2024; Vescio et al., 2008). Core to PLCs is the belief that professional learning is most effective when it takes place within a supportive community where educators share experiences, learn from each other, and solve problems together (Douglas, 2024). PLCs are also excellent structures through which to create networks of improvement communities (NICs) as part of improvement science (Woodland, 2016). In this way, PLCs focus on creating a culture of continuous improvement by fostering collaboration, shared leadership, and a commitment to enhancing student learning (Stoll et al., 2006).

The benefits of PLCs are well-documented in research and educational literature. PLCs have been shown to improve collective teacher efficacy and ultimately lead to better student outcomes (Lee et al., 2024; Linder et al., 2012; Voelkel & Chrispeels, 2017). Similarly, in their review of studies on PLCs, Vescio et al. (2008) found that participation in PLCs leads to improved teaching practices, increased teacher collaboration, and enhanced student learning. By providing a supportive environment where teachers can engage in reflective practice and collaborate on innovative solutions, PLCs foster a culture that prioritizes student learning and continuous improvement (De Jong et al., 2022). Stoll et al. (2006) emphasized that effective PLCs help build individual, group, and schoolwide capacity through shared norms, mutual support, and collaborative learning, enabling schools to sustain improvement efforts over time.

In addition to the benefits already discussed, PLCs provide further advantages that contribute to overall school improvement. PLCs help to break down the isolation that many educators experience by creating structured opportunities for collaboration and peer learning (Wullschleger et al., 2023). This collaboration can lead to greater consistency in instructional practices across classrooms, which in turn helps ensure that all students have access to high-quality learning experiences. Furthermore, PLCs contribute to professional well-being by providing emotional support and reducing stress through collective problem solving and shared responsibility (Watson, 2014). This supportive environment not only improves teacher satisfaction but also leads to lower turnover rates, which is beneficial for maintaining stability and continuity within schools (Stoll et al., 2006)

Research suggests that effective PLCs share several key characteristics that support their positive impact on teaching and learning. They are characterized by shared values and vision, which drive the work of the community and ensure alignment toward common goals (Vescio et al., 2008). Reflective professional inquiry is another critical component, allowing educators to engage in meaningful conversations about instructional practices, student learning, and challenges they face (Harris & Jones, 2010). Collective responsibility is an important characteristic of effective PLCs, where members take shared ownership of improving student outcomes (Stoll et al., 2006). Additionally, effective PLCs foster mutual trust and respect among participants, creating a supportive environment that encourages open dialogue and collaboration (Watson, 2014).

In sum, PLCs are excellent vehicles through which to implement an improvement science approach as they provide a natural setting for collective inquiry, reflection, and action (Harris & Jones, 2010). The collaborative nature of PLCs also supports the continuous cycle of improvement by creating space for educators to routinely engage in identifying areas for growth, trying out new teaching strategies, and evaluating their impact on teaching and learning (Stoll et al., 2006).

Lesson Study

Finally, an additional body of research that heavily informs the VITAL Collaboration framework covers lesson study. Lesson study is a highly effective approach to professional learning, originating in Japan, that has been increasingly adopted globally. In lesson study, teachers collaborate in cycles of planning, teaching, observing, and analyzing lessons that resemble the PDSA cycles of improvement science. This iterative process aims to improve instructional practices and enhance student learning outcomes (Murata, 2011). During lesson study, teachers typically work together to plan or tune a lesson. One teacher teaches while others observe, and then they collectively analyze the lesson to understand its impact on student learning (Sharrock & Challen, 2023). The reflective, data-driven nature of lesson study helps teachers to better understand student thinking and identify strategies that support effective learning (Follmer et al., 2024).

Lesson study contributes to building teacher confidence and efficacy by providing a supportive environment for collaborative inquiry into instructional practice. Teachers who engage in lesson study benefit from vicarious learning experiences, as they observe peers' instructional approaches and contribute to discussions on improving practice (van den Boom-Muilenburg et al., 2022). Furthermore, research suggests that leadership plays a critical role in sustaining lesson study as an ongoing practice, emphasizing the importance of supportive school environments that prioritize teacher learning (van den Boom-Muilenburg et al., 2022).

Lesson study also provides an opportunity for teachers to collaboratively plan, observe, and analyze lessons in real-time classroom settings. By engaging in lesson study within a PLC, teachers benefit from collective inquiry and shared expertise, which leads to more effective teaching strategies and improved student learning outcomes (Murata, 2011; Sharrock & Challen, 2023). The collaborative nature of lesson study also fosters a culture of continuous improvement, where teachers are encouraged to take risks, experiment with new approaches, and learn from one another (van den Boom-Muilenburg et al., 2022).

A SIMPLE THEORY OF IMPROVEMENT

As we mentioned earlier in this chapter, the research above can be synthesized into a simple Theory of Improvement that helps transform key concepts into a logical framework for action. To recap, the research highlights the importance of collective teacher efficacy for enhancing student achievement, the power of improvement science and its focus on feedback in facilitating systematic changes, and the role of PLCs in supporting reflective, data-driven collaboration. These foundational ideas provide the basis for a structured, strategic Theory of Improvement that empowers schools to elevate both teaching and student outcomes. See Figure 2.2.

Figure 2.2 synthesizes the research shared above into a practical Theory of Improvement. We find it easiest to explain this theory by working or mapping backwards, much as many teachers engage in backwards planning to design lessons. To begin, the last box describes the desired future state of any improvement in schools: positive outcomes for students. Working backwards, an unavoidable truth in education is that for the positive outcomes for students to come to fruition (i.e., increased learning and achievement), they must first be preceded by collective improvements in teaching. This is because, as mentioned above, collective teacher efficacy is one of the most important factors that influence learning. And as the common phrase goes, "Every system is perfectly designed to get the results it gets" (IHI Multimedia Team, 2015). Thus, if we want student learning to shift in a positive direction (i.e., improve), then these changes must be preceded by commensurate shifts or improvements in the teaching practices that influence student learning.

Continuing to work backwards, if we want the collective efficacy of teaching to improve, it in turn must be preceded by routine and iterative opportunities for teachers to receive feedback. As the research on improvement science demonstrates, improvement is optimized the more individuals can engage in productive feedback cycles. As described above, PLCs are places where teachers can make their teaching practice visible so as to receive

Figure 2.2. A Simple Theory for Improving Teaching and Learning

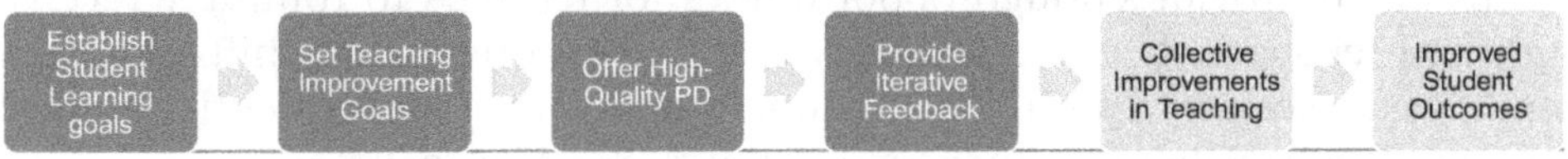

Figure 2.3. The Theory of Improvement Scale

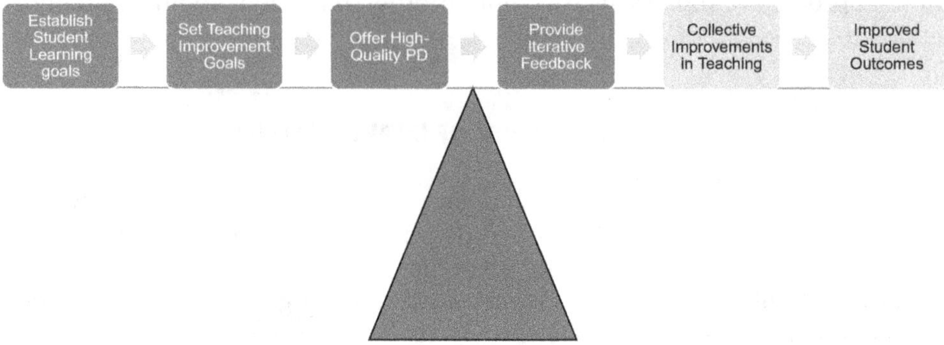

feedback from their colleagues. The more opportunities they have to engage in productive feedback, the more likely improvement will occur. Similarly, as the fourth box in Figure 2.2 emphasizes, feedback is optimized when it is grounded in and informed by what research indicates is best practice. Thus, when teachers have opportunities to engage in professional learning around best practices they are more likely to use this knowledge to inform the feedback that provide to colleagues in PLCs.

Finally, this brings us to the first two boxes. In short, as mentioned above, professional learning is most effective when it is geared to the needs of teachers and students. Thus, it is important for teachers to collectively set their own teaching improvement goals at the school, PLC, and personal level. These goals in turns are most effective when they are aligned with the goals that educators develop for student learning.

There is one more key point to make about this Theory of Improvement. Figures 2.3, 2.4, and 2.5 illustrate this. First, consider Figure 2.3. This graphic shows the Theory of Improvement in Figure 2.2 placed on the top of a fulcrum. It is intended to highlight the work needed to scale improvement. The last two boxes are shaded lighter because they are desired results and do not require work per se. When visualized in this way, we can see that there is a lot of work to do before teachers start receiving feedback. If the bulk of time is spent setting goals and engaging in PD, then the scales will be tipped away from the desired outcomes. See Figure 2.4.

Figure 2.4 shows what happens when the work in the first stages is disproportionate—the scale of improvement tilts to the left. We want to tip the scale the other way, toward the desired outcomes. The primary way to do this is to provide enough opportunities for teachers to routinely receive targeted feedback, because feedback is the main driver that shifts practices and tips the scale in a positive direction. In other words, it is essential to stack enough feedback loops to make a difference. See Figure 2.5.

Figure 2.4. Unbalanced Improvement

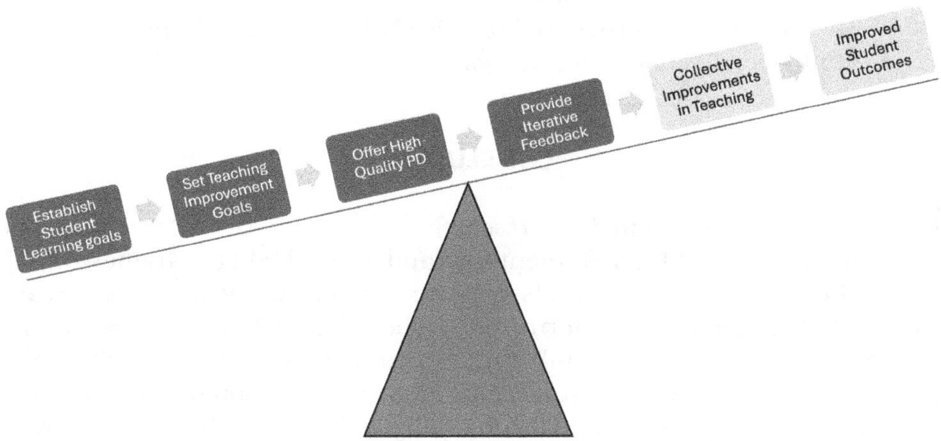

Figure 2.5. The Gravity of Feedback

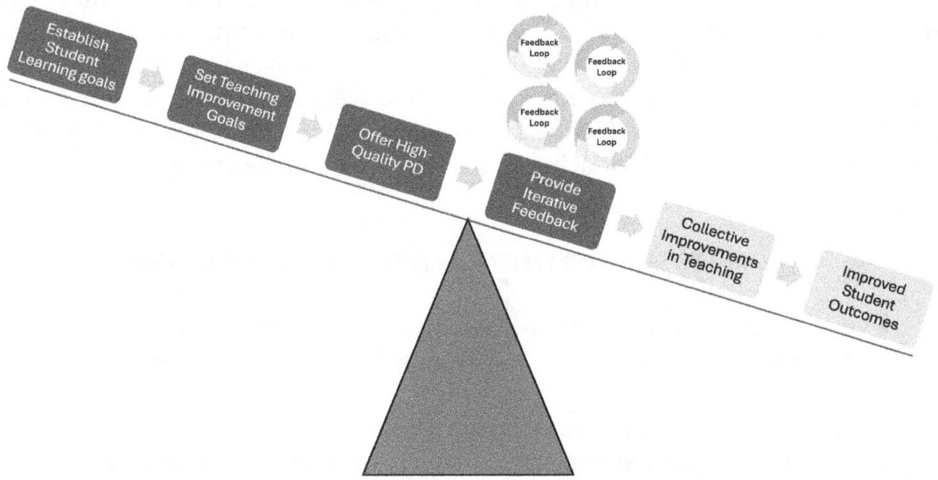

In sum, the Theory of Improvement we propose can be summarized in the following way.

- If we set clear and attainable learning goals for all students, and
- If we develop teaching improvement goals aligned with the student goals, and
- If we provide teachers with high-quality PD to help them achieve their teaching goals, and

- If we create opportunities to get routine feedback as teachers practice applying new ideas gained from PD,
- Then teachers' instructional practice will collectively improve, and
- Students will attain desired goals.

CONCLUSION

In this chapter, we outlined the research base for VITAL Collaboration and presented a Theory of Improvement that underpins the VITAL framework. To recap, effective collaboration is essential for enhancing teaching practices and student learning, but not all forms of collaboration yield the desired results. For collaboration to be impactful, it must focus deeply on improving teaching practices connected to student learning outcomes. It should also align with professional learning, sustained through ongoing feedback loops that provide teachers with actionable information to refine their instruction. Most importantly, it must be maintained over time to foster meaningful improvement.

With this foundational understanding of the research that supports VITAL Collaboration, the next chapter will dive deeper into the structure of the VITAL framework. You will learn how every element of the framework is designed to strengthen collective teacher efficacy and how it applies the Plan-Do-Study-Act (PDSA) cycle through its four phases. We will also explore how teaching and learning cycles create feedback loops and why focusing on instruction at the lesson level is crucial for achieving schoolwide improvement.

PROMPTS FOR FURTHER READING AND REFLECTION

- What did you learn or take away from reading this chapter? Identify 2–3 insights or key points that resonated with you and explain why they stood out.
- Summarize the key concepts from this chapter in your own words. How would you explain these concepts to a colleague or team member?
- In your current role or school setting, how does this chapter's content align with or diverge from your experiences? Identify 1–2 actionable implications for your context.
- What challenges do you anticipate in applying the ideas from this chapter to your work? How might you address or overcome these challenges?
- Briefly scan the next chapter you plan to read. What topics or themes do you anticipate, and what specific questions do you hope to answer as you read?

CHAPTER 3

The Architecture of VITAL Collaboration

A Framework for Success

PRE-READING PROMPTS

- Think about a time when collaboration with your colleagues led to significant improvements in your teaching practices. What made that collaboration successful, and how did it impact your students' learning?
- Reflect on the current state of collaboration within your school. In what ways do these efforts align with or diverge from your school's overall goals for student achievement?
- Consider the role of feedback in your collaborative efforts. How often do you receive actionable feedback from your peers, and how does it influence your instructional decisions?
- What are your expectations for VITAL Collaboration as a framework for improving both teaching practices and student outcomes? What do you hope to gain from implementing this approach in your school or district?
- What questions do you hope this chapter will answer? List 2–3 specific questions that you're curious about.

INTRODUCTION

In Chapter 2 we made a case for why routine collaboration focused on improving collective teacher efficacy is so important. We also highlighted research that suggests how to leverage collaboration to achieve these results, specifically employing an improvement science approach in PLCs that focuses on enhancing instructional practice at the lesson level. We concluded by synthesizing the research into a Theory of Improvement to help drive action.

In this chapter, we introduce the VITAL Collaboration framework. This is an approach we have developed to put the research shared in Chapter 2 into action. First we share an example of what VITAL Collaboration looks like in action. Then we provide an overview of the framework and describe its four key phases. We then discuss some of the features that make VITAL different from other approaches we frequently see schools take. We conclude by describing three key roles that are required for VITAL Collaboration to thrive and the responsibilities associated with each. Let's begin by looking at what VITAL looks like in action.

WELCOME TO INSPIRED HEIGHTS

Imagine stepping into Inspired Heights Community School on a crisp fall morning, as teachers prepare to meet in their grade-level professional learning communities (PLCs). The chill in the air mixes with the warmth of greetings exchanged in the hallways, and the smell of freshly brewed coffee drifts through the building. A positive energy is palpable in the air, a blend of purpose, collaboration, and shared commitment. Teachers move with focused enthusiasm, and you hear the murmur of conversations, punctuated by laughter and questions, as teams hustle to meet in classrooms scattered around the school. This is a school that lives and breathes VITAL Collaboration, where every member of the community is engaged in visibly improving teaching and learning.

You are joining the Grade 3 PLC today. It is the beginning of the semester and the focus for the meeting is on setting a student learning goal for the PLC. The teachers begin by reviewing the schools' goals on improving reading and math achievement. Next they look at student data and work samples they collected from recent assessments, spreading out colorful data charts and annotating them with bright markers as they discuss patterns and trends. As they look over their data, they identify areas where students are excelling and those where they are most ready to improve. The team decides to set a specific student learning target that aligns with one of their school's goals to improve students' math achievement: *improving students' ability to explain their mathematical reasoning*. Once the PLC target is set, the teachers collectively establish a SMART goal for their own collective practice: *to incorporate more targeted questioning techniques during math instruction to support deeper student explanations*. Throughout the meeting, the team is led by Ms. Rivera, the facilitator, who uses probing questions to ensure the goals are specific, realistic, and linked directly to student data and the school's goals and vision. You leave the meeting feeling impressed with the focus and precision of the team's work.

You return a few weeks later when the team is meeting to tune a lesson focused on improving students' math reasoning. One teacher, Mr. Patel, offers a draft lesson plan and projects it onto the screen. The group leans in, and they use a lesson tuning protocol to refine it, their voices overlapping as they ask questions, offer praise, give suggestions, and ultimately share their takeaways. Their discussion is rich, as colleagues offer insights and suggestions. "What if we include more think-write-pair-share opportunities to help students articulate their reasoning before sharing with the whole group?" suggests Ms. Green. "That was a really useful strategy I learned during the recent workshop we had." The group agrees, and they adjust the lesson to integrate this new idea. More ideas like this follow. By the end of the meeting, the team has provided Mr. Patel with a bunch of new ideas he is excited to try. Other members also comment that they intend to try some of the ideas in their own lessons as well.

The following week, Mr. Patel teaches the revised lesson while his colleagues observe. Although he appears a little nervous to have so many adults embedded in the class, you can see his confidence grow as the lesson progresses, and you are impressed with how he has seamlessly integrated many of the ideas from the last week's PLC into his teaching. As he teaches, his colleagues take careful notes, looking for evidence of student engagement and clarity of reasoning. Later in the day, they meet to analyze what they observed and learned. This is the third part of a teaching and learning cycle: analyzing student work. During this PLC, they analyze samples of student work from the think-write-pair-shares, and they celebrate successes, like the active student participation. They also identify areas to adjust, such as providing more scaffolding for students who need it.

Fast forward a few months, and the Grade 3 PLC is studying the results of their learning. They are meeting to examine recent assessment data and compare it to earlier benchmarks. The team is excited as the data shows growth; more students are better able to articulate their thought processes in math. The teachers reflect on their improved practice, discussing how their questioning techniques have evolved and sharing specific examples of how students have responded with greater depth and clarity. They document their findings and craft an email to share the results with school leadership, noting both the successes and areas for continued growth.

Toward the end of the semester, you get to witness multiple PLCs celebrate their learning journey at a whole-school staff meeting. During the meeting, the Grade 3 team presents their work and showcases student artifacts that highlight the growth made in mathematical reasoning. They describe the challenges they faced and the strategies that worked. The atmosphere is celebratory—not because the work is over, but because it represents a meaningful step forward in the teachers' collective journey of improvement. The room is filled with praise and words of encouragement, and you notice proud smiles as teachers exchange nods of recognition. You sense that the teachers feel empowered and that their collective effort contributes to a culture where learning and growth are celebrated.

As you reflect on what you have observed over the course of the semester and the multiple PLC meetings you sat in on, you realize that what you have witnessed at Inspired Heights is more than just a series of gatherings. What you have experienced is a deep and systematic commitment to using collaboration as a driver for improving teaching and learning. This shows in the quality of student work, in the reflective conversations among teachers, and in the culture of growth that is present in every visit.

* * *

The description above is a compilation of experiences we have had working with partner schools across the country building their capacity to implement the VITAL Collaboration framework. Reflect back on what you read. Did you notice that there were different phases to the collaboration as the school year progressed? If so, how would you describe them? Also, what did you observe about the kinds of activities that the Grade 3 PLC engaged in? How did these connect to each other? How were they different? How were they similar? Keep these questions in mind as we explain how VITAL Collaboration works.

VITAL COLLABORATION: AN OVERVIEW

As shared previously, VITAL Collaboration stands for "Visibly Improving Teaching and Learning Through Collaboration." This name pays homage to John Hattie's work around "visible learning" (e.g., Hattie, 2009, 2023; Hattie & Zierer, 2019), which emphasizes a key finding from his and his team's review of thousands of studies and meta-analyses: that learning is optimized when it is made visible. This is true for students. It is just as true for adult learners.

Although there have been criticisms of Hattie's work (e.g., McKnight & Whitburn, 2020; Nielsen & Klitmøller, 2021; Rømer, 2019), our review of the research, as well as our experience working in schools across the country, lead us to a similar conclusion: When individuals make their work visible for others, they create space for dialogue and discussion about it. In doing so, opportunities open for feedback and reflection, which in turn encourage growth and improvement.

Despite this finding, and as anyone who has ever walked into a school knows, most schools are not designed for visibility or transparency. For example, in many schools we work with, teachers are prohibited from recording videos of their instruction for policy or legal reasons. In addition, many teachers we collaborate with tell us they rarely get to see another teacher teaching or that they only infrequently have someone watch them teach and give constructive feedback. Therefore, to help making learning visible, VITAL Collaboration provides a structured framework that encourages teachers to make their professional practice visible to their peers so they can receive feedback. It leverages the power of improvement science, PLCs, and lesson study to do this. Let's now take a closer look at the framework and the kind of work it encourages teachers to engage in together in their teams.

THE FOUR PHASES OF VITAL COLLABORATION

Figure 3.1 illustrates the main components of VITAL Collaboration. As Figure 3.1 shows, VITAL is organized into four distinct phases, each of which plays a critical role in guiding teacher teams through a continuous cycle of improvement. You will note these four phases are consistent with the four phases of improvement science: plan, do, study, act. Below is a description of key activities we encourage PLCs to engage in during each phase. We also briefly introduce some of the protocols in each phase that are designed to help teachers engage in the collaborative work described. These protocols can be found in Part III of this book.

PHASE 1: PREPARING FOR TEACHING AND LEARNING CYCLES

The first phase of VITAL Collaboration focuses on laying the groundwork for effective collaboration. During this phase, teacher teams begin by establishing or reestablishing their team's working norms. The Protocol for Establishing PLC Norms in Part III helps them do this. Next, they use the Protocol for Setting Student Learning Goals to do just that. This begins with a thoughtful review of current student performance data to pinpoint areas where students are struggling or where there are gaps in their learning. The team then sets targeted learning goals for their students that are directly linked to these identified needs.

After setting student learning goals, teams develop teaching improvement goals. The Protocol for Developing Teaching Improvement Goals guides them through this process. Teaching improvement goals are typically centered around enhancing specific instructional practices that will help teachers better meet their students' needs. We encourage readers to recall the Theory of Improvement shared in Chapter 2. For example, a team might decide to set a goal that focuses on improving questioning techniques to promote deeper student thinking. Or, a team may establish a goal to strenghten their approach to differentiating instruction. The key is that these goals should be SMART—Specific, Measurable, Achievable, Relevant, and Time-bound—and that they are closely aligned with the overall objectives of the school.

Finally, Phase 1 concludes with teams preparing to engage in the teaching and learning cycles of Phase 2, in which PLC members will take turns sharing artifacts from various phases of their teaching: planning, teaching, and reviewing student work. In addition to this, during Phase 1, teams also

Figure 3.1. The VITAL Collaboration Framework

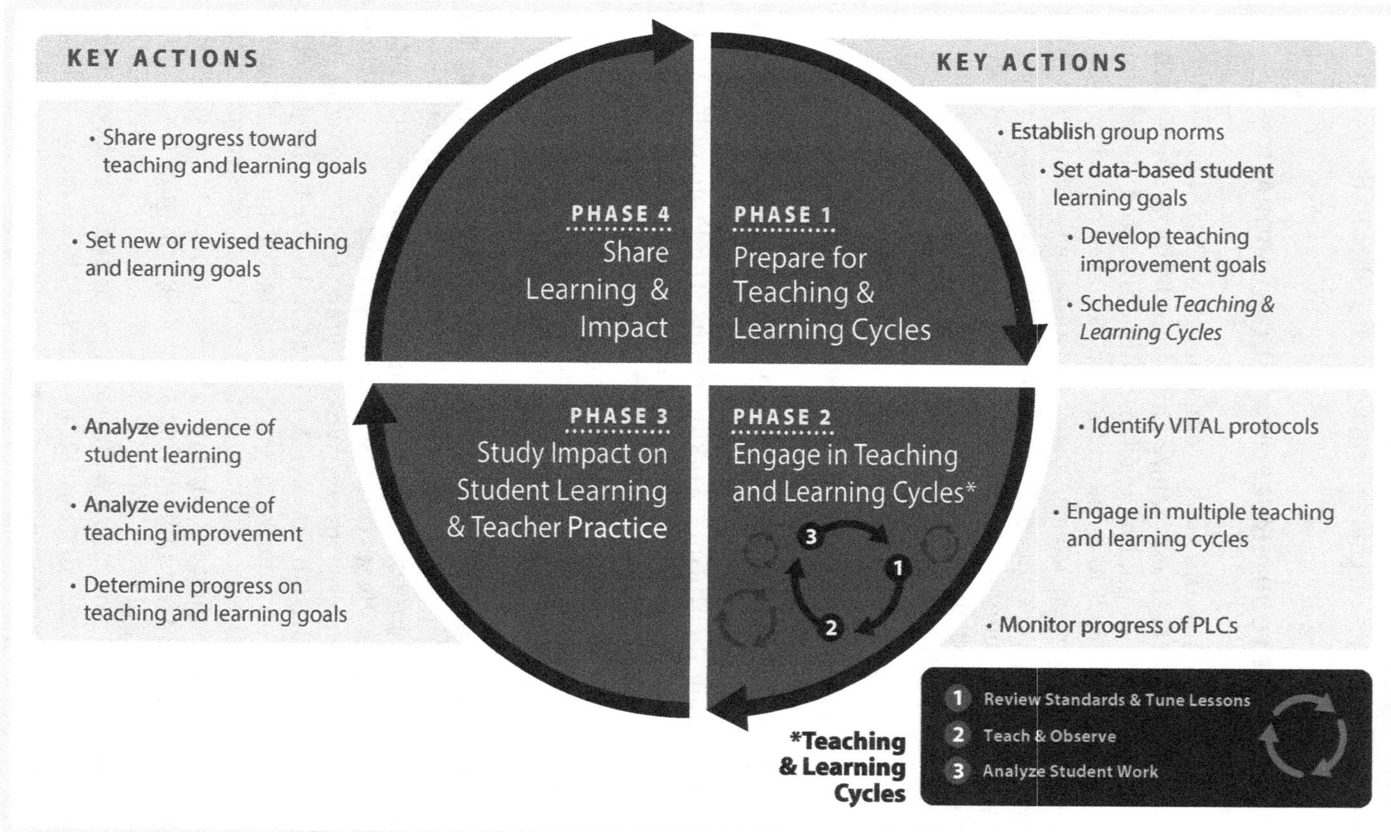

plan for the collection of new student data to serve as a baseline for assessing the impact of the collaborative efforts on student learning. Data will be collected to measure progress throughout the VITAL Collaboration process, ensuring that the team's work is grounded in evidence.

PHASE 2: ENGAGING IN TEACHING AND LEARNING CYCLES

Phase 2 is the heart of VITAL Collaboration. It is where the bulk of instructional improvement takes place. This is where PLCs should spend most of their time, as this is when the most feedback is generated. During this phase, teacher teams engage in multiple rounds of Teaching and Learning Cycles (TLCs), each of which usually involves conversations around the following: analyzing the focus standards of a lesson, lesson tuning, teaching and observing, and analyzing student work. To complete a TLC, PLCs dedicate a PLC meeting to each conversation type. For example, if a PLC meets weekly, it will most likely take them a month or more to engage in a complete TLC for a single teacher. We briefly summarize each type of conversation in a TLC below. Each also has a corresponding protocol in Part III.

Analyzing Standards

The first part of a teaching and learning cycle is analyzing the primary standard that will be the focus of a lesson to be tuned later. When analyzing standards, teams use the Protocol for Analyzing Standards to review a focus standard for a lesson or series of lessons that will be taught soon. It is not uncommon for standards to be complicated and dense, or for teachers to have differing opinions about what standards really ask for. By analyzing a standard together, the team generates a common understanding that can then be used to inform their teaching.

Tuning a Lesson

The TLC continues with a discussion where teachers use the Protocol for Tuning a Lesson to refine a lesson that addresses the standard previously analyzed and that aligns with the teaching improvement goal identified in Phase 1. We find that tuning lessons is essential, even when teachers are using instructional materials from resources developed by professional vendors. This is because most lessons still need to be modified or adapted to the specific students and context of a teacher's classroom.

During the lesson tuning process, a presenting teacher shares a lesson, particularly one through which they are striving to integrate new strategies or practices aligned with the teaching improvement goal. The teacher presents the lesson, identifies the type of feedback that would be most useful, and the PLC team then analyzes it to provide feedback, always beginning with praise. The collaborative nature of this process allows teachers to pool their expertise, share resources, and incorporate diverse perspectives to provide feedback. Lesson tuning conversations typically end with the team planning to observe the lesson being taught.

Teaching and Observing

Once the lesson is tuned, it is time for the presenting teacher to teach it and for PLC members to observe it. This observation can be done in real time, with teachers visiting each other's classrooms, or through video recordings that can be reviewed later. The focus during this step is on gathering detailed information about how the lesson unfolds, how students respond, and how effectively the instructional strategies are implemented. Observers take notes and use specific observation protocols to ensure that their feedback is focused and actionable.

Once the lesson has been taught, the team reconvenes and uses the Protocol for Discussing a Classroom Observation. During this conversation, the PLC reviews what kind of feedback the teacher who taught the lesson was looking for and then they share and analyze the data gathered during the lesson. This leads into a discussion of what went well and where there are opportunities for growth.

Analyzing Student Work and Learning

After the discussion and analysis of the instruction, the team reconvenes to analyze the results using the Protocol for Analyzing Student Work. This protocol walks the team through a structured process for reviewing student work and determining the extent to which students learned or mastered the key concepts and skills from the standard the lesson was focusing on. The team then uses this information to determine the implications and next steps for instruction.

When considering the four areas of conversation involved during the teaching and learning cycle—standards, lesson design, teaching, and student work—it is important to reiterate that the purpose of each is to generate feedback related to core teaching practices associated with each conversation. For example, when analyzing standards, teachers get feedback about how they are interpreting and planning to apply their understanding of academic standards. During lesson tuning they receive feedback on the design of lessons they intend to teach. Within the observation step, teachers get feedback on their actual instruction. Finally, when teams analyze student work, the student work itself provides information about what students learned and what teachers might benefit from addressing next. It is through the feedback generated from these steps of a teaching and learning cycle, and by stacking multiple cycles together, that enough feedback is generated to collectively shift the teaching practice of the entire PLC.

PHASE 3: STUDYING IMPACT

After completing several TLCs, PLC teams transition to Phase 3, where they focus on studying and measuring the impact of their collaborative efforts. This phase begins with the collection or gathering of new student data, which is then compared to the baseline data gathered in Phase 1. The goal is to assess whether the changes in teaching practices have led to measurable improvements in student learning. In addition to analyzing student outcomes, teams also reflect on the changes in their instructional practices. This reflection is crucial for understanding how specific strategies contributed to the observed outcomes and for identifying areas where further improvement is needed. By systematically studying the impact of their work, teacher teams can ensure that their collaborative efforts are leading to tangible, positive changes in the classroom. To assist teams with these conversations, Part III of this book includes the Protocol for Monitoring Progress of Teaching and Learning.

PHASE 4: SHARING AND CELEBRATING LEARNING

The final phase of VITAL Collaboration involves acting on the insights gained during the previous phases. This includes documenting the results of the collaborative process and sharing them with key stakeholders, such as colleagues, school leaders, and even the broader community. Sharing results not only helps to build a culture of transparency and accountability but also allows other teachers to learn from the experiences of the team and to adopt successful strategies in their own practice. Phase 4 also emphasizes the importance of celebrating successes and recognizing the hard work of the team. By acknowledging the progress made, schools can foster a sense of collective achievement and encourage ongoing commitment to the collaborative process. As with the other phases, a protocol for sharing and celebrating teacher learning is provided in Part III.

KEY FEATURES OF VITAL COLLABORATION

In many schools, professional learning communities have become a staple of collaborative practice. However, despite the widespread adoption of PLCs, we often see these initiatives fall short of their potential. Too often, PLCs become routine meetings where process overshadows substance, goals lack alignment with broader school objectives, or data is misunderstood and misused. These challenges can lead to frustration among educators, making the promise of collaboration seem unattainable. The problem is not the concept of PLCs themselves but how they are implemented. Below, we highlight some of the features of VITAL that are designed to mitigate or address many of the challenges we encounter with PLCs and many of the other approaches to collaboration we frequently encounter in schools.

Alignment to School Goals

One of the most significant challenges with traditional PLCs is that their efforts can become disconnected from the overarching goals of the school. VITAL Collaboration ensures that every collaborative effort is purposefully aligned with schoolwide objectives. This alignment is not just about checking a box; it is about creating a coherent strategy where every PLC is contributing to the broader vision and goals of the school. By doing so, VITAL fosters a unified approach to professional development and student achievement, ensuring that the time and energy spent on collaboration are directly contributing to the school's mission.

Use of Structured Protocols

One of the biggest insights we have gained over the years is the importance of using structured protocols to improve professional practice. For conversations to be impactful, they must be rigorous enough to encourage teachers to shift or improve their practice. This does not happen by accident, and conversations that do this cannot be replicated without a deliberate and structured approach. Thus, we have developed over time a suite of protocols designed to provide the necessary structure for fostering conversations that drive improvement. We provide these protocols in Part III. We also begin that part of the book with a chapter that describes the intentional design of the protocols, so facilitators know how and why the protocols are organized the way they are.

Intense Focus on Iterative Feedback

In many collaborative settings, feedback can be vague, unfocused, sporadically given, or even absent. VITAL Collaboration prioritizes actionable feedback that is directly tied to the goals set by the team. This feedback is not only essential for individual growth, but also critical for ensuring that the entire team is moving forward in a cohesive and productive manner. By centering feedback on specific, observable practices, VITAL Collaboration helps teachers refine their instruction in ways that are immediately applicable and measurable. This focus on feedback transforms collaborative sessions from mere discussions into powerful opportunities for professional growth that help to improve collective teacher efficacy.

Grounded in Standards

VITAL Collaboration emphasizes the importance of grounding discussion and analysis of instruction in academic standards. By using standards as a foundation, teacher teams can ensure that their instructional practices are not only aligned with best practices but also with the specific expectations for student learning in their subject areas. This grounding in standards helps to maintain the relevance and rigor of the collaborative work, ensuring that it has a direct impact on classroom instruction and student outcomes. Teachers are encouraged to align their lesson planning, instruction, and assessments with these standards, creating a consistent and high-quality learning experience for all students.

KEY ROLES: SCHOOL LEADERS, PLC FACILITATORS, TEACHERS

The success of VITAL Collaboration also hinges on the effective collaboration between three key roles within the school: school leaders, PLC facilitators, and teachers. Each role is vital to the overall process, with distinct responsibilities that, when carried out effectively, support the collective goal of improving teaching and learning. We describe each of these roles and some of their most important responsibilities below.

School Leaders

School leaders, including principals, administrators, leadership teams, and instructional coaches all play a crucial role in setting the vision and providing the support necessary for VITAL Collaboration to thrive. In the companion book *A School Leader's Guide to VITAL Collaboration*, we dive more deeply into the roles and responsibilities of all school leaders in supporting VITAL Collaboration. However, here we emphasize that they are responsible for establishing a culture of collaboration within the school, ensuring that time and resources are allocated for PLCs to meet regularly and meaningfully. School leaders must also communicate the importance of alignment between PLC activities and schoolwide goals, making sure that every collaborative effort contributes to the broader vision for student achievement.

To fulfill this role, school leaders need to be well-versed in the principles of VITAL Collaboration and understand how to facilitate and support the work of PLCs. They should provide ongoing professional development opportunities, model collaborative behaviors, and be actively involved in the PLC process without dominating it. School leaders also need to ensure that PLC facilitators have the training and resources they need to be effective in their roles. By fostering a supportive environment, school leaders help to remove barriers to collaboration, making it easier for PLCs to focus on improving teaching and learning.

PLC Facilitators

The teacher leaders who facilitate PLCs in schools are at the heart of the VITAL Collaboration process. If leaders are the keystones keeping the structure in place, then facilitators are the mortar that binds the collaborative efforts into a strong and enduring whole. They are the ones who hold their teams together and guide them through each phase of the collaboration cycle, ensuring that the work remains focused, data-driven, and aligned with school goals. They are also the ones to facilitate the protocols provided in Part III. Because of its critical importance, the role of the PLC facilitator is both challenging and rewarding, requiring a deep understanding of the collaborative process, strong leadership skills, and the ability to foster a positive and productive team dynamic. Part II of this book is dedicated to building the skills and capacity of teacher leaders to be effective PLC facilitators.

To be effective, facilitators need to be knowledgeable about instructional practices, data analysis, and effective collaboration strategies. They must be able to lead discussions that are focused on improving teaching and learning, ensuring that every meeting is purposeful and productive. Facilitators are also responsible for maintaining the momentum of the PLC, keeping the team on track with their goals, and helping to navigate any challenges that arise.

One of the most important aspects of the PLC facilitator's role is to create a safe and supportive environment where all team members feel valued and heard. This involves encouraging open and honest communication, managing conflicts constructively, and ensuring that feedback is both given and received in a way that promotes growth. Facilitators must also be adept at using data to inform the team's decisions, helping to demystify the data analysis process and ensure that it is used effectively to drive instructional improvements.

The PLC facilitator also must work closely with school leaders and teachers, serving as a bridge between the two. They ensure that their team's work is aligned with the school's goals while also advocating for the needs and concerns of the teachers. By supporting the PLC facilitator in their role, school leaders help to create a culture of continuous improvement, where collaboration is not just encouraged but embedded in the fabric of the school.

PLC Members

Teachers are the core participants in the VITAL Collaboration process. Their active engagement and membership in their PLC will determine the extent to which a PLC will achieve its goals of improving teaching for student learning. To that end, teachers must be willing to bring their classroom experiences, instructional expertise, and student data to the table, making the collaborative process rich and relevant. Their active involvement ensures that the collaborative work is directly connected to the realities of teaching and learning in their specific context.

It is essential that teachers be open to giving and receiving feedback, willing to engage in reflective dialogue, and committed to the continuous improvement of their practice. They play a key role in setting and achieving the goals of the PLC, bringing their unique perspectives and insights to the collaborative process. By actively participating in VITAL Collaboration, teachers contribute to the development of a professional culture that values growth, accountability, and shared responsibility for student success.

In summary, the roles of school leaders, PLC facilitators, and teachers are interdependent, each supporting and enhancing the work of the others. School leaders provide the vision and support, PLC facilitators guide the process, and teachers bring the essential content and context that make collaboration meaningful. Together, these roles create a powerful nexus for improving teaching and learning through VITAL Collaboration.

CASE STUDIES OF VITAL COLLABORATION

To help illustrate what VITAL Collaboration might look like in different educational contexts, we now introduce three fictional schools as case studies to support further inquiry and understanding of VITAL Collaboration: Sunnyside Elementary School, Valley View Middle School, and Riversedge High School. As mentioned earlier, we will use these three schools in Parts I and II to demonstrate what many of the key concepts presented in each chapter look like in action. However, it is important to note that the case studies are not intended to be perfect examples of every facet of VITAL Collaboration. Therefore, as you read, free to compare some or all of the schools to your own context, and how you might approach things the same or differently.

Sunnyside Elementary School: Using VITAL Collaboration to Improve Literacy Instruction

Welcome to Sunnyside Elementary School, a vibrant community serving diverse young learners from varied cultural and socioeconomic backgrounds. With a significant portion of its student body identified as English Language Learners, the school prioritizes literacy as a foundational skill. Sunnyside's vision highlights literacy as essential for academic and life success; this vision guides its instructional practices and professional learning efforts. To achieve it, the school has set ambitious goals focused on reading comprehension and language development, aiming to ensure that every student meets or exceeds grade-level literacy standards. Recognizing the need for a structured approach to collaboration, the school's principal introduced VITAL Collaboration as a solution. Here is a high-level summary of one PLC team's experience with this approach.

At the start of the school year, the 1st-grade team faced a persistent challenge: a significant number of students were struggling with phonemic awareness, a foundational skill crucial for reading success. Despite various interventions, progress remained slow, and teachers were concerned about the long-term impact on students' reading abilities.

The team began their collaborative journey by engaging in Phase 1 of VITAL Collaboration, where they gathered and analyzed student data to identify specific areas of need. They discovered that while some students were making progress in other areas of literacy, phonemic awareness remained a consistent gap. This data-driven insight allowed them to set targeted goals focused on improving this specific skill.

In Phase 2, the team participated in multiple teaching and learning cycles. Each teacher took turns presenting a lesson plan centered on phonemic awareness, which the group refined using the Lesson Tuning Protocol. They observed each other's lessons, either live or through video recordings, and used structured feedback sessions to discuss effective strategies and areas for improvement. For instance, one teacher introduced a new phonics game that quickly became a favorite among students. Through collaborative discussion, the team decided to incorporate this game into their schoolwide instructional plans.

By Phase 3, nearing the end of the first semester, the team evaluated the impact of their efforts. New assessments showed significant improvements in students' phonemic awareness, with a higher percentage of students meeting grade-level benchmarks. The final phase, Phase 4, involved sharing these results with the broader school community. The 1st-grade team presented their findings during a staff meeting, highlighting both successes and challenges. Their experience with VITAL Collaboration not only improved literacy outcomes but also fostered a stronger, more cohesive team dynamic.

Valley View Middle School: Using VITAL Collaboration to Enhance Inquiry-Based Science Learning

Meet Valley View Middle School, a school dedicated to fostering inquiry-based learning across its curriculum, particularly within its STEM and social studies programs. Valley View has a diverse student body with strong representation from several ethnic and socioeconomic groups. The school's vision emphasizes nurturing critical thinking and problem-solving skills, encouraging students to explore and question deeply. This vision is supported by schoolwide learning goals that prioritize mastery of scientific inquiry, mathematical reasoning, and historical analysis. With the introduction of VITAL Collaboration, educators have begun working together in PLCs to design and refine inquiry-focused lessons, review student work, and assess progress toward shared academic goals, ensuring each student is prepared for future academic success. Below is the story of the Science Department's PLC.

The Science Department at Valley View faced a common middle school challenge: students were often disengaged during science lessons, especially with inquiry-based activities. The department head observed that while teachers valued inquiry-based learning, its implementation varied across classrooms. Some teachers excelled at engaging students, while others struggled to foster deep engagement. To address this inconsistency, the department leaned into the VITAL Collaboration framework to bring uniformity and effectiveness to their approach.

In Phase 1, the science teachers analyzed student performance data and noticed a concerning trend: students were underperforming on assessments that required critical thinking and problem-solving—key skills for inquiry-based learning. Using this data, the team set a goal to improve student engagement and mastery of these skills through enhanced inquiry-based instruction.

During Phase 2, the teachers engaged in a series of TLCs, collaboratively planning and observing each other's inquiry-based lessons. For instance, one teacher developed a lesson on ecosystems where students created their own mini-ecosystems and made predictions about changes in the environment. The team provided feedback to refine the lesson, such as adding opportunities for students to pose their own questions and conduct experiments. These observations and discussions underscored the importance of scaffolding the inquiry process for students who were less confident, leading to new strategies that were adopted across all science classes.

By Phase 3, new data indicated that students were more engaged in science lessons and performing better on critical thinking assessments. Teachers observed that students were asking more questions and taking greater ownership of their learning. In Phase 4, the department shared their findings with school leadership and other departments, sparking schoolwide discussions on how inquiry-based learning could be expanded to other subjects. The Science Department's success with VITAL Collaboration provided a model for other departments to follow, fostering a culture of continuous improvement throughout the school.

Riversedge High School: Using VITAL Collaboration to Address Achievement Gaps in Algebra

Welcome to Riversedge High School, located in an urban setting and committed to closing achievement gaps in core subjects, particularly in algebra. This gateway subject opens doors to higher-level math and STEM opportunities, making it a critical focus area for the school. With a diverse population that includes a high percentage of students from groups historically underrepresented in STEM, Riversedge's vision emphasizes equitable access to rigorous academic content, empowering all students to succeed in mathematics and beyond. The school's learning goals center on improving algebra proficiency, aiming for every student to build the skills needed to advance to higher math courses. To support this vision, faculty members at Riversedge have begun using VITAL Collaboration protocols to analyze data, identify effective instructional strategies, and develop targeted interventions that support struggling students. Below is an account of the Algebra I team's experience with VITAL Collaboration.

The Algebra I team at Riversedge faced a familiar challenge: while some students excelled in Algebra I, many others—especially those from underserved backgrounds—struggled to meet grade-level expectations. The math department recognized that addressing this achievement gap was essential but felt that previous attempts lacked the coordination and consistency needed for meaningful progress. They turned to VITAL Collaboration to structure their efforts.

In Phase 1, the Algebra I team thoroughly analyzed student data, including standardized test scores, classroom assessments, and attendance records. They identified that the gap stemmed not only from challenges with algebraic concepts but also from low student confidence and engagement. With this understanding, the team set dual goals: to improve students' mastery of key algebraic concepts and to boost their confidence in mathematics.

During Phase 2, the team participated in Teaching and Learning Cycles (TLCs) focused on making algebra accessible and engaging. One teacher introduced a flipped classroom model, where students watched instructional videos at home and used class time for guided practice and peer problem-solving. The team observed and provided feedback on this approach, discussing ways to ensure that all students, particularly those struggling, could keep up with the material. Another teacher experimented with real-world applications of algebra to help students see the relevance of what they were learning, which significantly increased engagement.

In Phase 3, the team reviewed the impact of these new approaches. They were thrilled to see a marked improvement in student engagement and performance. Previously disengaged students were now participating actively, and their test scores showed a deeper understanding of algebraic concepts. Although the achievement gap wasn't entirely closed, it had narrowed significantly.

In Phase 4, the math department shared their results with the broader school community, including the school board and parents. They presented their findings at a districtwide professional development day, demonstrating how VITAL Collaboration had transformed both student outcomes and the department's approach to teaching algebra.

CONCLUSION

In this chapter you gained a foundational understanding of what VITAL Collaboration is and how it is designed to transform teaching and learning through structured, purposeful collaboration across four phases of collaboration. We explored the foundational concepts, the phases of the VITAL process, particularly the teaching and learning cycle, and the ways in which this approach addresses common challenges in traditional PLCs.

As we move forward, the next section of the book will take a deeper dive into the role of PLC Facilitators, whom we consider to be the driving force behind successful collaboration in PLCs. We will explore how facilitators can effectively guide their teams through the VITAL process, manage group dynamics, and ensure that every meeting is productive and aligned with schoolwide goals. You'll learn about the key skills and strategies that make facilitators successful, along with practical tips for overcoming challenges they might face.

PROMPTS FOR REFLECTION AND DISCUSSION

- Consider the narrative of Inspired Heights. How did the description of collaborative endeavors in the narrative compare to you own experiences?
- How does the concept of VITAL Collaboration differ from other collaborative practices you have experienced?
- What elements of VITAL Collaboration resonate the most strongly, or which are most familiar? Which were the least familiar or most surprising?
- How do you anticipate the VITAL process could help address the challenges you currently face in your school or PLCs?
- What steps can you take to begin implementing VITAL Collaboration in your school or district?

Part II

GUIDANCE FOR PLC FACILITATORS

In Part II of this book, we focus on equipping PLC facilitators with knowledge and skills essential for leading PLCs and implementing the VITAL Collaboration framework. This section dives into the core characteristics of effective facilitation and provides strategies for navigating common challenges and for building the capacity of facilitators to lead high-quality collaborative efforts. By strengthening these foundational skills, facilitators will be better prepared to guide their PLCs through the protocols discussed in Part III, ultimately driving improvements in teaching and learning. Below is a brief overview of the three chapters in this part of the book.

Chapter 4, "Becoming an Effective PLC Facilitator: Essential Qualities and Roles," explores the core beliefs and key roles of an effective facilitator; these roles include Vision Keeper, Safety Provider, and Instructional Leader. Understanding these roles is crucial for facilitators to build trust and maintain focus within their teams.

Chapter 5, "Mastering Facilitation: Core Practices for Impactful Collaboration," delves into practices like attentive listening, strategic questioning, and the use of depersonalized language. These techniques foster meaningful dialogue and create an environment conducive to continuous improvement. Mastering these skills will help facilitators effectively lead their teams in reflective discussions and collaborative problem solving.

Chapter 6, "Overcoming Obstacles: Addressing Challenges in Facilitation," addresses obstacles such as resistance, time constraints, and lack of leadership support. It provides strategies to overcome these hurdles, ensuring that PLCs remain focused and productive. This chapter equips facilitators with tools to manage the complexities of leading collaborative efforts, enhancing their ability to drive sustained improvements.

By the end of Part II, facilitators will have a solid foundation in many of the skills necessary to guide their teams through effective collaborative practices, setting the stage for implementing the protocols in Part III.

CHAPTER 4

Becoming an Effective PLC Facilitator

Essential Qualities and Roles

PRE-READING PROMPTS

- Reflect on past experiences you have had collaborating with colleagues in PLCs or other collaborative settings.
  - » Who led or facilitated this collaboration?
  - » What did they do in their role as facilitator?
  - » What beliefs do you think they had about professional learning?
  - » How were the beliefs enacted?
- What would you consider to be important defining characteristics of an effective facilitator or team leader?
- What do you think are the core responsibilities of an effective PLC facilitator?
- What core beliefs do you think it is essential for PLC facilitators to have?
- To what extent do you believe each of the following statements are true?
  - » A shared vision unites and drives effective PLCs.
  - » Safety and trust are essential for effective collaboration.
  - » Structured processes optimize conversations about improvement.
  - » Collaboration is essential to collective improvement.
  - » Equity and inclusivity optimize a PLC's potential.
  - » Facilitators are instructional leaders.

INTRODUCTION

To effectively facilitate a professional learning community that can routinely meet its potential of improving teaching and learning, it is important for teachers who are leading conversations with their colleagues to have a foundational set of beliefs from which to work. These beliefs help to define the responsibilities facilitators need to shoulder. In turn, these responsibilities shape the knowledge and skills facilitators need to do the work of collaborating to improve. Strong facilitation is critical to the success of PLCs, yet it presents significant challenges, especially when facilitating peers who are also colleagues. Unlike traditional leadership roles, PLC facilitators are often teachers themselves, which necessitates a delicate balance of peer leadership and camaraderie. This dance is not easy to master.

This chapter provides a foundation of what we have found makes a strong PLC facilitator. We begin by highlighting six core beliefs that we strongly believe underpin effective facilitation. We then briefly summarize the key responsibilities associated with these beliefs that define the role of an effective PLC facilitator. Understanding these elements is crucial for facilitators who wish to lead their teams toward meaningful collaboration that has the potential to transform teaching practice and improve student outcomes.

CORE BELIEFS

Facilitating a PLC effectively starts with having an appropriate mindset. This mindset includes having core beliefs that shape how facilitators approach their roles and responsibilities. These beliefs inform the responsibilities facilitators shoulder and the actions they take. They also help facilitators create environments where collaboration can thrive. This sets the stage for fostering meaningful discussions and achieving impactful outcomes. Below we highlight six of these beliefs. As you read about each, consider the extent to which you agree with it and how you might put the belief into action in your own collaborative work.

Belief 1—A Shared Vision Unites and Drives Effective PLCs

Effective facilitators understand that PLCs should align with the broader mission of the school. Ideally, each PLC meeting should contribute to the overarching goal of improving teaching practice and enhancing student learning and achievement (DuFour & Eaker, 1998). Consider Sarah, a facilitator at a midsized elementary school. Every time her PLC meets to discuss instructional strategies, she begins by referencing the school's vision and goals. One afternoon, as the team wrestled with implementing a new math curriculum, Sarah brought the conversation back to their shared goal: improving student numeracy. She said, "Remember, our work here isn't just about getting through the curriculum. It's about equipping our students with the skills they need to thrive in the next grade level and beyond." This reminder helped the team refocus on the bigger picture, allowing them to evaluate lessons in the curriculum and their alignment with their long-term goals. By consistently connecting their work to the school's vision, Sarah ensured that every decision the team made was purposeful and aligned with broader objectives.

A simple strategy a PLC facilitator can take to help ensure alignment of the team's work with the school's vision and goals is to have the PLC team create their own vision that is nested within that of the school. We sometimes call this a "little v" vision. For example, consider the following sample school vision: *Our school is committed to nurturing well-rounded individuals who excel academically, think critically, and contribute positively to society.* Below are examples of PLC-level or "little v" visions for content-specific PLCs that align with the larger school vision.

- Our Math PLC aims to improve how we help all students understand and confidently apply math in real life.
- Our Literacy PLC is dedicated to strengthening our teaching practice to foster a love for reading and writing in every student.
- Our Science PLC seeks to routinely inspire curiosity and develop critical thinking through hands-on learning.

Belief 2—Safety and Trust Are Essential for Effective Collaboration

A second belief of effective facilitators is the importance of prioritizing safety and trust. This belief is a cornerstone of any successful collaboration. For collaboration to be effective, facilitators must foster an environment where team members feel safe to express ideas, share challenges, and take risks without fear of judgment. This assertion is backed by a body of research which has found that trust within teams is essential for open communication and innovation (Edmondson & Bransby, 2023). For example, consider John, a high school science teacher who recently stepped into the role of PLC facilitator. In one of the first meetings he led, a veteran teacher hesitated to share a concern about her classroom management. John noticed her hesitation and immediately shifted the tone of the meeting. "We're here to support each other," he said, "and that means being honest about what's not working as well as what is." He then shared a personal story about a time he struggled with a similar issue, effectively opening the floor for others to share their challenges. By modeling vulnerability, John created a safe space where teachers felt comfortable discussing their struggles, leading to more honest and productive conversations.

One of the most effective and important approaches PLC facilitators can take to promote a strong sense of safety and trust is to work with the PLC's members to develop strong working norms and working agreements. Later in this book we provide tools and protocols for helping facilitators develop and maintain these. A few examples of norms and working agreements we have experienced that help establish safety and trust include the following: maintain confidentiality, listen attentively, be present, and value all voices.

Belief 3—Structured Processes Optimize Conversations About Improvement

A third belief that it is important for facilitators to embrace is the role structured conversations play in driving conversations about improvement. Both research and our experience indicate that effective facilitation requires structured processes, such as protocols, to guide discussions and maintain a focus on a team's goals (e.g., McLaughlin & Talbert, 2006). Structure is crucial because conversations about teaching practice need to be rigorous enough to have the potential to transform instruction. Simply talking about our teaching practice is typically not enough to routinely bring about improvement. We must thoughtfully analyze it, consider what is working, identify areas for improvement, and determine the steps needed to foster growth. This level and depth of reflection does not happen by accident; it is achieved only through structured discourse.

A common concern we hear when introducing protocols to PLCs during coaching and training workshops is that using protocols implies that a team cannot have a conversation independently. However, for conversations to truly improve teaching, we have found that they must follow a specific sequence of steps to be deep enough to prompt meaningful shifts in how teachers approach their work. Consider Maria, for example. She is a facilitator at a large urban middle school, who noticed that her PLC meetings often veered off track, leaving little time for reflection and feedback. To address this, she introduced a protocol for analyzing and discussing student work. The protocol included specific steps: First, a teacher would present student work without commentary, followed by a period of silent observation. Then, a structured discussion focusing on evidence rather than opinion took place. The first time the PLC used the protocol, Maria observed a significant shift. The conversation became more focused and encouraged every teacher to contribute meaningfully. By the end of the meeting, the team had developed a clear action plan to address some of the gaps that were observed in student understanding. This structured approach not only kept the meeting on track; it also ensured that the discussion led to actionable outcomes.

Belief 4—Collaboration Is Essential to Collective Improvement

Perhaps it goes without saying, but another core belief that facilitators must genuinely have is valuing collaboration as a tool for improving teaching practices and enhancing student outcomes. Much of this is summarized in Chapter 2 of this book. For example, this belief is evident in the approach taken by David, an experienced facilitator at a suburban high school. David was known for his ability to bring out the best in his team by encouraging diverse perspectives. During one of our visits to his PLC, we observed a particularly challenging discussion about implementing differentiated instruction. As the conversation evolved, David noticed that a few teachers were dominating the conversation. He paused the discussion and said, "We have a lot of expertise in this room, and I'd like to hear from those who haven't spoken yet. What challenges or successes have you experienced with differentiation?" This simple prompt brought new voices into the conversation, leading to a richer discussion. By actively seeking out and valuing different perspectives, David was able to better foster a culture of collaboration where every member felt their contributions were important.

Belief 5—Equity and Inclusivity Optimize a PLC's Potential

Another core belief is the need to ensure that every voice is heard and valued during a PLC. In other words, facilitators need to value and work actively to promote the voices of all members. A PLC will not reach its full potential until it is able to leverage the wisdom of all members (Nieto, 2010). For example, this commitment to equity was central to the approach taken by Lisa, a facilitator in a diverse elementary school. Lisa noticed that some of her team members, particularly novice staff and those from underrepresented groups, were hesitant to share their perspectives during meetings. To address this, she implemented a "round-robin" discussion format, where each teacher had the opportunity to speak without interruption, as well as the option to pass. Additionally, she made it a point to follow up with quieter members after meetings to gather their input and ensure their voices were included in the final decisions. Over time, we noticed Lisa's team become very inclusive and balanced, with every member actively contributing to the discussions on a routine basis. By creating a space where all voices were valued, Lisa helped her team develop more comprehensive and innovative solutions to the challenges they faced.

Belief 6—Facilitators Are Instructional Leaders

The last belief we wish to highlight is the importance of facilitators viewing themselves as instructional leaders who play an essential role in guiding and supporting their colleagues in their improvement efforts. As Robinson, Lloyd, and Rowe (2105) found, the more leaders, including teacher leaders, focus their efforts on improving instruction, the greater their influence on student outcomes. This does not mean that facilitators are expected to "know it all" or always be knowledgeable about best practice, but it does mean they should emphasize the value in always striving to learn more and to model the ways to strengthen one's own practice. This was effectively demonstrated by Salman, a PLC facilitator in a rural high school. Salman was passionate about integrating technology into the classroom and regularly brought new tools and resources to his team. One day, after attending a conference on digital learning, Salman shared a presentation on using formative assessment apps to engage students in real-time feedback. He didn't just stop at sharing the tools; he also led a hands-on session where he and his colleagues could explore the apps and discuss how they might be used in their own classrooms. Salman's enthusiasm and leadership inspired his colleagues to experiment with new technologies, ultimately leading to improved student engagement and learning outcomes.

ROLES AND RESPONSIBILITIES

The core beliefs described above significantly inform the roles and responsibilities that effective PLC facilitators shoulder. Considering all the above, we encourage facilitators to embrace the following roles as leaders of their team. We also summarize some of the responsibilities that go along with each role. In the next chapter we go deeper into essential practices that help facilitators fulfill these responsibilities across the various roles.

Vision Keeper

As Vision Keepers, facilitators are responsible for ensuring that the PLC's work is consistently aligned with the broader goals of the school and the team's own shared vision. This role is grounded in the belief that a shared vision unites and drives effective PLCs. Facilitators in this role help the team stay focused on long-term goals by regularly revisiting the school's mission and how the PLC's objectives contribute to it. For instance, a facilitator might begin each meeting by linking the discussion to the school's overarching aim of improving student outcomes, reminding the team of the bigger picture and their collective purpose. By maintaining this focus, Vision Keepers ensure that every action taken by the PLC is purposeful and aligned with their shared objectives, driving meaningful progress.

Safety Provider

As a Safety Provider, facilitators are responsible for creating a psychologically safe environment where all PLC members feel comfortable expressing their thoughts, ideas, and concerns. This role directly ties to the belief that safety and trust are essential for effective collaboration. Facilitators embody this responsibility by establishing and upholding norms that promote confidentiality, respect, and attentive listening. For example, facilitators might start each meeting by revisiting these norms and encouraging members to speak openly about their challenges without fear of judgment. Through consistent actions and modeling, Safety Providers ensure that every member feels valued and supported, leading to more honest, productive, and innovative discussions that drive collective improvement.

Team Manager

PLC facilitators play a pivotal role in ensuring that PLC meetings are purposeful, efficient, and supportive of teacher growth. This requires effective team management in a number of areas. Below are some of the key responsibilities that PLC leaders undertake to effectively manage their teams.

- *Set agendas:* Work to ensure that every meeting is planned with a focused agenda that provides direction and purpose for the team's work. End meetings by determining the agenda for the next meeting.
- *Organize materials:* Take responsibility for gathering and organizing materials required to keep conversations productive.
- *Set roles and norms:* Clarifying roles such as timekeeper or note-taker, along with reviewing group norms, helps create accountability and ensures meetings stay on track.
- *Clarify purpose:* Articulate the specific goals for each meeting sets at the outset.
- *Focus on standards*: Standards provide a common language and a goalpost for discussions, which the PLC facilitator uses to keep inquiry focused on effective teaching and learning.
- *Encourage reflection:* Allocate time at the end of meetings for reflection on process, which helps the team understand what worked well and what could be improved.

In sum, effective PLC facilitators work to ensure that PLC meetings are well-organized and focused on growth, utilizing clear agendas, structured processes, and reflective practices to foster effective collaboration and continuous improvement.

Protocol Leader

As Protocol Leaders, facilitators are often tasked with implementing structured processes that guide the PLC's discussions and decision-making. This role aligns with the belief that structured processes optimize conversations about improvement. Facilitators ensure that meetings are focused and productive by introducing and adhering to protocols that structure the flow of conversation. These protocols help the team maintain a rigorous approach to analyzing teaching practices and student outcomes, ensuring that every discussion leads to actionable insights. For instance, a facilitator might use a protocol for examining student work, where the team follows specific steps to objectively evaluate the work and develop strategies for improvement. By providing this structure, Protocol Leaders keep the PLC on track and ensure that discussions remain purposeful and outcome-oriented.

Conversation Guide

As Conversation Guides, facilitators are responsible for navigating the dialogue within the PLC to ensure that all voices are heard and that the conversation stays on track. This role reflects the belief that collaboration is essential to collective improvement. Facilitators must be adept at managing the flow of discussion, knowing when to intervene to bring in quieter voices or refocus the conversation when it strays off-topic. For example, a facilitator might notice that a few members are dominating the discussion and pause to invite others to share their perspectives. By actively managing the conversation, Conversation Navigators ensure that every member's input is valued, leading to richer, more inclusive, and ultimately more effective collaborative efforts.

Continuous Learner

As Continuous Learners, facilitators model a commitment to ongoing professional development and encourage their PLC members to do the same. This role aligns with the belief that facilitators are instructional leaders who should continuously strive to improve their own practice. Facilitators demonstrate this responsibility by actively seeking out new knowledge, resources, and strategies that can benefit the team. For example, a facilitator might share insights from a recent workshop or introduce a new teaching tool they have been experimenting with in their own classroom. By leading by example, Continuous Learners inspire their colleagues to adopt a mindset of growth and continuous improvement, which is essential for sustaining the momentum of the PLC and achieving long-term success.

Instructional Leader

As Instructional Leaders, facilitators take on the responsibility of guiding and supporting their colleagues in improving teaching practices and student outcomes. This role is intimately connected to the belief that facilitators are instructional leaders who play a critical role in influencing educational practices within their teams. Facilitators embody this role by staying informed about the latest instructional strategies and modeling a commitment to continuous professional growth. For example, a facilitator might introduce new pedagogical approaches during PLC meetings and lead discussions on how these strategies can be implemented in the classroom. By actively contributing to the professional development of their peers and fostering a culture of continuous learning, Instructional Leaders help their PLCs become catalysts for instructional innovation and improvement.

CASE STUDIES

Let's now return to the three case studies from Chapter 3. Each story offers a vivid illustration of how different PLC facilitators bring to life the core beliefs and responsibilities we've discussed in this chapter. As you read through these narratives, try to spot the various beliefs and responsibilities in action. Consider how each facilitator navigates enacts the beliefs above, along with their role and responsibilities. Think about the impact their approach has on their teams and potentially their students.

Sunnyside Elementary: Breaking Down a Literacy Standard

Building on their success in phonemic awareness, the 1st-grade PLC gathered one crisp morning, surrounding a table filled with notebooks, student work samples, and freshly sharpened pencils. Mrs. Martinez, the facilitator, warmly welcomed each teacher, her steady presence creating a comfortable atmosphere. "Today, let's focus on one standard in depth," she began. "We'll use the Analyzing Standards Protocol to break it down and make it accessible for every learner."

Mrs. Martinez had chosen a specific standard: CCSS.ELA-LITERACY.RF.1.2, Demonstrate understanding of spoken words, syllables, and sounds (phonemes). She introduced the standard by writing it on the whiteboard and reading it aloud, inviting the teachers to reflect. "What does 'demonstrate understanding' look like in practice?" she asked, encouraging each teacher to visualize student success. Together, they broke down the knowledge and skills within the standard.

The teachers then shared observations of their students' current abilities related to this standard. Ms. Price mentioned a group who could identify syllables but struggled to isolate sounds within words. Mrs. Martinez listened thoughtfully and asked, "What kinds of activities have you tried to support them so far?" This open-ended question allowed teachers to share strategies without judgment, fostering a safe space for reflection.

As they moved into the discussion phase, Mrs. Martinez encouraged practical suggestions for meeting the standard, reminding them to keep the language of the standard in mind. "If 'demonstrate understanding' is our goal, what specific steps can we use to get them there?" she prompted. This focus helped the teachers think of achievable milestones rather than feeling overwhelmed by the end goal.

The team brainstormed ideas, from tapping out sounds with fingers to using visual and tactile aids, with Mrs. Martinez occasionally redirecting the conversation to students' needs. When Ms. Rios expressed concern about reaching students who struggled more than others, Mrs. Martinez nodded empathetically. "Let's think about how we can create access points for all students," she suggested. "What's one way we might start with smaller steps for those who need extra support?" This reframing led to a lively exchange of differentiated activity ideas to support various learning levels.

By the end, the teachers felt grounded in their approach to the standard, having mapped out specific activities to scaffold students' understanding of syllables and sounds. Mrs. Martinez wrapped up with encouragement. "We're all aiming toward the same goal, and every small step counts," she said, instilling a sense of shared purpose. "Let's try one new activity this week and bring back what we observe." The team left with a clear plan and renewed unity, reminded by Mrs. Martinez that even small adjustments could make a meaningful difference in students' literacy journeys.

Valley View Middle School: Elevating Inquiry-Based Learning

On a damp Thursday afternoon, Valley View's 7th-grade science PLC gathered around a table covered with lesson plans, data charts, and steaming cups of coffee. The room buzzed with shared excitement as they prepared to refine a lesson on mini-ecosystems. Mr. Garcia, the facilitator, opened the meeting with a welcoming invitation for everyone to share their ideas. "Let's build on what each of us brings today," he said, smiling. "We all have different insights to contribute."

As they moved into the Protocol for Tuning a Lesson, Mr. Garcia explained each step with care, ensuring all teachers felt comfortable. Ms. Tran was the first to share her approach, describing how she would guide students in observing food chains within their mini-ecosystems. Mr. Garcia listened thoughtfully and asked, "What could we add to encourage students to think about the 'why' behind their observations?" This question sparked a rich discussion, with each teacher contributing questions to encourage connections between observation and reasoning.

During feedback, Mr. Garcia encouraged everyone to start with positive observations, emphasizing what was working well. Each teacher's ideas were met with affirming nods and thoughtful responses, creating a supportive space. When Ms. Tran shared her plan to use "think-alouds" to model scientific explanation, Mr. Garcia leaned in and encouraged her. "That's a great approach," he noted. "What challenges do you anticipate?" This question led to a collaborative brainstorming session on making think-alouds accessible for students needing extra support.

By the end of the meeting, the team had crafted a lesson that fostered curiosity and empowered students to articulate their scientific thinking. Mr. Garcia closed with a gentle reminder: "Today, we've strengthened our own teaching, and through that, we're helping our students find their voices in science." The team left feeling inspired and energized by both the refined lesson and the collective spirit that shaped it.

Riversedge High School: Closing Algebra Achievement Gaps

Welcome back to Riversedge High School, where the Algebra I PLC is working diligently to close achievement gaps in algebra. At a recent meeting, the team gathered around data sheets and samples of student work. Mr. Carter, the facilitator, set a tone of empathy and purpose, reminding the team, "Our goal today is to understand each student's learning journey and identify ways to support them." His steady voice encouraged the team to view each student's challenges as opportunities for growth.

Using the Protocol for Analyzing Student Work, Mr. Carter guided the discussion with structured prompts. Ms. Reynolds shared work samples highlighting specific student challenges and growth points. Mr. Carter encouraged the team to start by focusing on students' strengths, fostering a safe and constructive environment. "This student is beginning to grasp the structure," he observed, redirecting attention to progress rather than mistakes. "What might help them connect the next steps?" he asked, leading to a productive discussion on supportive questioning techniques, including visual aids and prompts to help students articulate their problem-solving steps.

As they examined additional samples, Mr. Carter encouraged the team to consider ways to support students needing extra foundational help. "How can we make sure these strategies work for all students?" he asked, sparking a discussion on scaffolding and adapting prompts to meet diverse needs. The team left the meeting with concrete strategies, confident in their collective insights to support every student.

The session ended with a renewed sense of purpose, as teachers felt both supported and empowered. Through a collaborative and structured approach, they developed strategies to bridge achievement gaps and ensure each student had a path to success in algebra.

CONCLUSION

In Chapter 4, we explored the essential beliefs and roles that effective PLC facilitators bring to their work, showcasing how these guiding principles influence the work that transpires in PLCs. Through beliefs such as fostering a shared vision, ensuring a safe and inclusive environment, and maintaining a commitment to equity, facilitators lay the groundwork for meaningful, sustained improvement in teaching and learning. We recognize that these roles require facilitators to wear many hats and that people are naturally stronger in some areas than others. Thus, we encourage facilitators to revisit this chapter periodically to hone those areas most primed for growth.

As we move forward to Chapter 5, we will delve into the specific facilitation practices and techniques that bring these beliefs and roles into daily PLC work. The next chapter offers practical guidance on active listening, strategic questioning, and other essential skills that enable facilitators to lead productive discussions, foster reflective dialogue, and build a collaborative environment. By mastering these techniques, facilitators will be able to more effectively support their teams in achieving their goals and addressing challenges, setting the stage for impactful and continuous improvement.

QUESTIONS FOR FURTHER REFLECTION AND DISCUSSION

- Reflect on your experiences as a facilitator. How have your beliefs influenced your approach to leading a PLC?
- What beliefs presented in this chapter resonate most strongly with you? Which do you find the most challenging?
- Consider a recent PLC meeting you participated in as either a facilitator or member. How were the roles and responsibilities described in this chapter embodied?
- What steps can you take to enhance psychological safety within your PLC?
- In what ways can you strengthen your role as an Instructional Leader in your PLC?
- What are some ways PLC leaders can model continuous learning?
- What beliefs and practices did you observe through the case studies? What impact do you think they had on their PLCs?

CHAPTER 5

Mastering Facilitation

Core Practices for Impactful Collaboration

PRE-READING PROMPTS

- Reflect on your previous experiences in facilitating or participating in PLCs. What specific practices, or moves, do facilitators make that contribute to the effectiveness of these collaborative efforts?
- What specific knowledge or skills do you hope to gain from reading this chapter? How might these help you in your role?
- How do you currently approach facilitation in your professional setting? Which practices do you prioritize, and why?
- Consider the challenges you have witnessed in PLCs. How might refining certain facilitation practices help overcome these obstacles?
- What questions do you hope this chapter will answer? List 2–3 specific questions that you're curious about.

INTRODUCTION

In the previous chapter, we explored the foundational beliefs, roles, and responsibilities that define an effective PLC facilitator. This chapter builds on those foundations by delving into specific functions and practices that bring a PLC to life. Here, we outline the core functions of a PLC facilitator's role as well as essential practices that enable them to fulfill these responsibilities effectively. As we discussed, the aim of any PLC is to ensure that each teacher leaves the meeting better equipped than when they arrived. This requires facilitators to cultivate an environment where teachers feel safe, supported, and motivated to engage deeply with their own and each other's practices.

The practices covered in this chapter—ranging from attentive listening to creating space for constructive feedback—are designed to help facilitators bridge the gap between current teaching practices and a shared vision for improvement. By embracing these, facilitators empower their teams to navigate rigorous conversations, foster a collaborative culture, and make impactful changes in their teaching. We'll also examine how these practices align with the VITAL framework's emphasis on making our learning visible and creating feedback loops, ensuring that the facilitation process itself models the kinds of reflective, inquiry-based practices we hope to foster in our classrooms. Let's begin by examining the three core functions that lie at the heart of effective PLC facilitation.

THE THREE CORE FUNCTIONS OF A PLC FACILITATOR'S JOB

Effective facilitation in a PLC requires a clear focus on what is being facilitated and why. The most impactful PLCs are those that actively improve or transform teaching practices within the group. This transformation is achieved by fostering deep, thoughtful, and rigorous conversations into our professional practice that support continuous adult learning. The goal is simple yet ambitious: to create a PLC environment where every teacher leaves each meeting with enhanced teaching skills. Achieving this level of improvement necessitates robust and rigorous conversations that can drive instructional transformation. We recognize that this is a high bar, and to meet it, facilitators need to embrace three core functions central to their role.

Facilitating a Common Understanding of Effective Teaching Practice

First, facilitators need to guide their PLCs toward a clear and shared understanding of what effective teaching in their context looks like. Without this shared understanding, it becomes challenging for members to align their improvement efforts. This understanding should be both specific and aligned with the school's vision and goals. For instance, if a school is focusing on enhancing students' listening comprehension, the PLC needs to have a clear grasp of evidence-based practices for effectively teaching this skill.

Facilitating a Shared Understanding of Current Teaching Practices

Facilitators also help teams gain a precise understanding of their current teaching practices. Using the example above, PLC members not only need to know what high-quality instruction for listening comprehension entails, but they also need to understand how their current practices compare to this ideal. This type of gap analysis helps PLCs identify areas for improvement, with facilitators playing a key role in guiding reflective discussions that allow teachers to assess their practices accurately.

Facilitating a Collective Commitment to Improvement

Finally, in addition to helping their PLCs develop a shared understanding of both the desired and current states of teaching practice, they must also work with their team to foster a collective commitment to improving. In short, effective facilitators cultivate a willingness among team members to bring their instructional practices closer to the ideal. Understanding what excellent teaching looks like and knowing where one stands in relation to it are only beneficial if there is a genuine desire to improve.

In summary, effective facilitation in PLCs revolves around consistently engaging team members in discussions that close the gap between current practices and a vision of improvement. All the protocols shared in Part III help facilitators do this. For example, the goal-setting protocols for Phase 1 help PLCs identify how they want their teaching practice to improve and to set goals to help get there. In addition, the protocols for the teaching and learning cycles in Phase 2 are specifically designed to foster a PLC's commitment to improvement. By using these resources, facilitators can support their colleagues in making actionable decisions that enhance their teaching. Given these three core functions, we now explore six specific practices facilitators use to foster conversations capable of driving improvement.

ESSENTIAL FACILITATOR PRACTICES

Effective PLC facilitation relies on specific practices that foster a collaborative and reflective environment where conversations are rigorous enough to drive instructional improvements. Figure 5.1 introduces these practices and provides a quick description. Each practice is described more fully below.

Practice #1: Attentive Listening

Attentive listening is foundational to facilitating well. This type of listening can go by many names, such as listening closely or listening actively. The core idea here is listening that focuses on what others are saying and not on what we are thinking. It encourages an outward mindset. Research by Nichols and Straus (2021) underscores that listening attentively not only enhances understanding but also fosters trust and openness within a group. In addition, according to Covey's *The 7 Habits of Highly Effective People* (2020), empathetic listening, or listening with the intent to understand, is crucial in building strong, collaborative relationships.

Listening closely to what colleagues say is a cornerstone of successful PLCs. When facilitators truly listen, they create a space where participants

Figure 5.1. Six Key Facilitation Practices for PLCs

Practice	Description
Attentive Listening	• The act of genuinely listening to others. It builds trust, signals respect, and creates space for all voices, fostering psychological safety and encouraging meaningful participation.
Appreciative Inquiry	• An approach that focuses on strengths rather than deficits. It promotes a positive atmosphere by building on what works, creating momentum and optimism for improvement.
Strategic Questioning	• The use of well-crafted questions to guide discussions. It stimulates critical thinking and reflection, prompting participants to consider new ideas and explore alternative strategies.
Reflective Dialogue	• The practice of examining experiences, celebrating successes, and learning from challenges. It helps participants analyze their practices constructively, supporting continuous growth.
Constructive Feedback	• Feedback that is specific, timely, and actionable. It drives professional growth by helping refine practices and reinforce a culture of improvement.
Depersonalized Language	• Language that focuses on ideas and practices rather than individuals. It ensures discussions are safe, supportive, constructive, and centered on collective improvement.

feel valued. This fosters trust and encourages increased engagement and more meaningful contributions from members. Additionally, listening carefully helps facilitators pick up on nuances and identify any underlying concerns that might not be immediately obvious. Attentive listening also enables facilitators to model the reflective practices they wish to cultivate, such as encouraging participants to listen to each other with the same level of attentiveness. Below are some suggested techniques to help facilitators listen attentively.

- *Focus on the Speaker*: Maintain eye contact, nod, and use other nonverbal cues to show engagement.
- *Make Sure People Are Finished Speaking Before Responding*: Avoid interrupting. Let the speaker finish their thoughts before responding.
- *Paraphrase*: Summarize what the speaker has said to confirm understanding. This is also called looping. Examples of ways to begin this technique is to say something like, "What you are saying is . . ." or "To clarify, you are saying that. . . ."
- *Ask Clarifying Questions*: Encourage deeper exploration of ideas by asking the speaker to elaborate. Simple prompts for this are "Can you tell us more about that?" or "What else?"

Practice #2: Appreciative Inquiry

Appreciative inquiry is a strengths-based approach that focuses on identifying what works well within a group to drive growth and improvement. Cooperrider, Stavros, and Whitney (2008) argue that by focusing on strengths rather than problems, groups are more likely to generate innovative solutions and maintain a positive, forward-thinking mindset that encourages collaboration and avoids blaming. This approach contrasts with traditional problem-solving methods, which often focus on deficits and can lead to a negative or a defeatist attitude. Appreciative inquiry encourages facilitators to guide discussions toward what the group does well, thereby creating a more energized and motivated team. Additionally, research suggests that when groups focus on their strengths, they are more likely to experience sustained improvement and greater resilience in the face of challenges (Bushe, 2012).

As an example, recall that we stressed the importance of PLC members having a clear understanding of their current and their desired teaching practices and a commitment to bringing collective practice closer to the ideal. A deficit-based approach would emphasize what teachers are not doing well or frame analyzing the difference between current practice and the ideal as inspection of what they are doing wrong. Appreciative inquiry takes an asset-based perspective by focusing on strengths and how teachers' practice does align with the ideal. Where there are differences between current practice and ideal practice, an asset-based approach would then seek to identify opportunities for learning and growth. Below are techniques that can help facilitators practice appreciative inquiry.

- *Use Positive Language to Frame Questions*: Ask questions that highlight successes, such as "What went well in this lesson?", "How can we build on our strengths?", "Where does our current practice align with what research indicates is most effective?"

- *Celebrate Achievements*: Regularly acknowledge and celebrate the growth, learning, and successes of the group. This also includes celebrating taking risks or trying something new, even if it does not go as well as hoped. Taking risks and trying something new should be celebrated, not avoided.
- *Translate Deficit-Based Language Into Asset-Based Language*: Redirect negative or problem-focused discussions toward constructive, strengths-based conversations. For example, a teacher might say the following during a PLC meeting: "I am not good at integrating technology into my lessons." A strong facilitator would hear that and say, "What I hear you saying is that you are working hard to develop your skills at integrating technology. This is worth celebrating!" Notice how this response uses paraphrasing to translate a deficit-based mindset into an asset-oriented one and makes it something to celebrate.
- *Create a Culture of Positivity*: Regularly integrate appreciative inquiry into meetings to cultivate a positive, solution-focused environment. Be on the lookout for deficit-based language and practice translating into positive language that is asset-oriented.
- *Model Appreciative Inquiry*: Demonstrate appreciative inquiry by consistently highlighting the strengths of the team and its members.
- *Provide Training*: Offer workshops, provide training sessions, or engage in group readings on appreciative inquiry to help all group members adopt and strengthen this mindset.

Practice #3: Strategic Questioning

Strategic questioning is a critical tool for deepening discussions and fostering reflective thinking. For example, Dalessio (2019) emphasizes that well-crafted questions can guide teachers toward deeper understanding and promote self-reflection that enhances teaching practice. Effective questioning encourages participants to think critically about their practices, to examine underlying assumptions, and to explore alternative approaches. Research by Walsh and Sattes (2016) shows that strategic questioning also helps to create a culture of inquiry within PLCs, where members are continually learning from one another and challenging themselves to grow. By asking the right questions, facilitators can help the group move beyond surface-level discussions to engage in meaningful analysis and problem-solving. The following are techniques facilitators can use to leverage the power of strategic questioning.

- *Use Open-Ended Questions*: Encourage exploration by asking questions that cannot be answered with a simple "yes" or "no." For example, instead of asking if a teacher was planning a warm-up activity at the beginning of class, one might ask the following: "What are some strategies that would engage students at the beginning of class and prepare them for deeper learning?"

- *Probe for Deeper Understanding*: Follow up on responses with questions like "Can you tell us more about that?", "What led you to that conclusion?", "What did you observe students doing and saying?"
- *Encourage Multiple Perspectives*: Ask questions that invite different viewpoints, such as "How might others see this situation differently?" or "How do you think your students would describe the activity?"
- *Develop a Bank of Questions*: Create a list of strategic questions in advance that might be tailored to a PLC's focus areas during a meeting.
- *Practice Questioning Techniques*: Regularly practice formulating and asking strategic questions to enhance your facilitation skills. Encourage all members to practice this type of questioning.
- *Seek Feedback*: After meetings, ask group members if the questions posed helped to deepen their understanding and engagement. Ask what questions were the most helpful.

Practice #4: Reflective Dialogue

Along with the practices described above, the use of reflective dialogue also helps to foster a culture of continuous learning within PLCs. According to Schön (1994), reflective practice involves critically examining one's own experiences to learn and improve. Thus, reflective dialogue refers to discourse that works in the same manner. Facilitators play a key role in promoting reflective dialogue by encouraging participants to think deeply about their teaching practices, the challenges they face, and the outcomes they observe. Additional research (e.g., Dogan et al., 2019; Jay & Johnson, 2002) indicates that reflective dialogue not only enhances individual learning but also strengthens the collective knowledge of the group. By creating opportunities for reflective dialogue, facilitators help teachers move beyond simply sharing ideas to engaging in meaningful analysis and synthesis of their experiences. All of the protocols in Part III encourage reflective dialogue as part of their design. Below are strategies facilitators can use to foster this type of discourse in their meetings.

- *Use Reflection Prompts*: Begin and end meetings with prompts that encourage participants to reflect on their recent experiences, such as "What have you learned from your last teaching experience?", "What did you take away from today's conversation?", or "What is one thing you can bring back to the classroom and try?"
- *Encourage Peer Feedback*: Facilitate discussions where participants provide feedback on each other's reflections, offering new insights or alternative perspectives. Encourage participants to identify the

strengths in each other's work, to ask strategic questions, and to suggest things to try out.
- *Create a Safe Space for Reflection*: Ensure that the environment is supportive and non-judgmental, allowing participants to share openly.

Suggestions for Strengthening This Practice:

- *Incorporate Regular Reflection Time*: Dedicate specific time during each meeting for reflective dialogue and for providing feedback. This is the heart of many of the protocols shared later in this book.
- *Provide Reflective Journals*: Encourage participants to keep a reflective journal to document their learning journey as a teacher, as well as thoughts and learning generated throughout the PLC process.
- *Model Reflective Practice*: Share your own reflections with the group to demonstrate the value of this practice. Much like think-alouds are powerful strategies in the classroom, they work well in PLCs as well.

Practice #5: Constructive Feedback

As discussed earlier in this book, constructive feedback is a vital component of fostering professional growth within PLCs. Hattie and colleagues (e.g., Hattie & Timperley, 2007; Wisniewski et al., 2020) argue that feedback is one of the most powerful influences on learning and achievement, but it must be timely, specific, and actionable to be effective; we would also add asset-oriented and kind. It should be given in a safe space where there is established trust. Facilitators must create an environment where feedback is seen as a tool for improvement and a pathway to growth rather than criticism. To this end, research by Kluger and DeNisi (1996) suggests that feedback that focuses on behavior rather than the individual is more likely to be accepted and acted upon. Additionally, feedback is most effective when framed in a way that encourages recipients to reflect on their practices and consider how they can make improvements. According to Stone and Heen in their book *Thanks for the Feedback* (2015), asking for permission before providing feedback creates a more receptive environment. When a person is ready and willing to receive feedback, they are more likely to process it constructively. For example, many of the protocols in Part III deliberately ask participants to name the type of feedback they want before it is given. Asking permission shows respect for the teacher's autonomy and can help reduce defensiveness. Below are a handful of techniques facilitators can use to encourage constructive feedback that is more likely to have the desired impact.

- *Seek Permission and Request a Feedback Focus*: If engaging in an analysis of teacher practice during a PLC, ask teachers if they would like feedback, and if so, what kind of feedback would be the most helpful. This creates a permission structure and helps focus feedback from members in that direction.

- *Be Specific and Timely*: Encourage feedback that is focused on specific behaviors or practices and offer it as soon as possible after the observation. Many of the protocols shared later, such as the lesson tuning protocol, build this into the process.
- *Balance Positive and Constructive Feedback*: Ensure that feedback includes both recognition of strengths and suggestions for improvement. See description of appreciative inquiry above. Another way to think about this is to sandwich constructive feedback within something positive. In other words, begin and end with praise.
- *Encourage Self-Assessment*: Before providing feedback, ask participants to assess their own performance to encourage self-reflection. For example, encourage them to identify their strengths and where they have opportunity to grow.
- *Establish Feedback Norms*: Create group norms that outline how feedback should be given and received to ensure it is constructive and supportive.
- *Provide Feedback Training*: Offer training sessions on how to give and receive feedback effectively to build the group's capacity in this area.
- *Use Feedback Protocols*: Implement structured protocols or organizers for providing feedback to ensure it is delivered in a consistent and productive manner. End meetings by asking what feedback was the most helpful.

Practice #6: Depersonalized Language

Depersonalizing language is another key practice effective facilitators use that is crucial for maintaining a focus on ideas and practices rather than on individuals. This helps to prevent defensiveness and works to promote a collaborative atmosphere. In our experience, it can also be one of the more challenging practices to master, along with appreciative inquiry. Research by Stone et al. (2023) emphasizes that the way feedback is communicated can significantly impact how it is received. Using depersonalized language allows facilitators to address issues without unintentionally triggering defensiveness or damaging relationships within the group. This approach is particularly important when discussing areas for improvement, as it helps to keep the conversation focused on professional growth rather than misperceived personal shortcomings. By maintaining a neutral and objective tone, facilitators can ensure that discussions remain constructive and focused on the shared goal of improving teaching and learning.

Below is an illustration of depersonalized language being used when providing constructive feedback. The illustration has three examples. The first example uses deficit-based and personalized language. The second example uses appreciative inquiry or asset-based language but is still personalized. The third example is both asset-oriented and depersonalized.

- *Personalized and Deficit-Based*: "You didn't include enough interactive activities in your lesson, which led to lower student engagement. You need to work on improving this to keep the students more involved."
- *Personalized and Asset-Based*: "You used some strong instructional strategies in your lesson. You could increase student engagement by incorporating more interactive activities. This would help you maintain the positive momentum you've already established."
- *Depersonalized and Asset-Based*: "The lesson included strong instructional strategies. Student engagement could be enhanced by incorporating more interactive activities. This could help maintain positive momentum already established."

When comparing the three examples, notice how the first example begins with the words "You didn't. . . ." For most people this would immediately raise their hackles. Even though the second example is not accusatory, it is still very personalized, which can encourage a listener to take the feedback personally and construe it negatively. Notice how the third example focuses on the lesson and actions that could improve. Out of the three examples, the third approach is most likely to be more effective. Just as we did for the other practices, below are suggestions for how facilitators can practice this technique.

- *Focus on the Task, Not the Person*: Frame feedback around the task or behavior rather than the individual, e.g., "The lesson plan could benefit from . . ." rather than "Your lesson plan needs . . ."
- *Use "We" Language*: Encourage collective responsibility by using phrases like "We might consider . . ." instead of "You should . . ."
- *Avoid Labels*: Refrain from using labels that might be perceived as judgmental or negative.
- *Practice Neutral Language*: Practice using depersonalized language in various contexts to make it a natural part of your facilitation style. It is all too easy to use personalized language, so encourage PLC members to notice it and, when it is noticed, practice rephrasing.
- *Role-Play Scenarios*: Use role-play exercises with group members to practice giving and receiving depersonalized feedback. Create examples of personalized language and work together to rephrase using depersonalized language.

- *Review and Reflect*: After meetings, reflect on the language used and consider how it could be further depersonalized for future discussions.

CASE STUDIES

Below we revisit the Sunnyside Elementary, Valley View Middle, and Riversedge High to illustrate the practices in action. As you read, consider which functions and practices each facilitator is demonstrating and how. Also, how do these narratives compare to experiences you have had?

Sunnyside Elementary School: Cultivating Student Engagement in Reading

With foundational literacy standards broken down, the 2nd-grade PLC at Sunnyside Elementary shifted to fostering student engagement in reading. Ms. Turner, the facilitator, introduced the Protocol for Setting Student Learning Goals. Early in the meeting, she encouraged the team to share recent data and insights from reading activities. As each teacher spoke, Ms. Turner listened attentively, nodding thoughtfully and jotting notes, signaling her openness to their perspectives. When Mr. Chen shared that some students seemed hesitant during group readings, she gently asked, "What strategies have you noticed that help make reading feel inviting for them?"

This question led Mr. Chen to reflect on informal approaches he'd tried, and another colleague shared her experience with paired reading, describing how it helped students build confidence before reading aloud. Ms. Turner encouraged the team to consider adapting this approach for their classrooms, guiding the discussion toward their objective by asking, "How could we measure the impact of paired reading on student engagement?" With considerable interest in this strategy, they began crafting a SMART goal focused on increasing the percentage of students reading aloud in a supportive setting.

As the meeting concluded, Ms. Turner summarized key action steps and affirmed each teacher's contribution, leaving the group encouraged and empowered to track and share their progress in future meetings. They left with a concrete goal and a shared responsibility to create a more engaging reading environment.

Valley View Middle School: Enhancing Inquiry-Based Learning Through Reflective Dialogue

At Valley View Middle School, the 7th-grade science PLC gathered to refine a lesson on the scientific method shared by Ms. Rivera. Facilitator Mr. Holt began the meeting by introducing the Protocol for Tuning a Lesson, setting a collaborative tone by revisiting their group norms. The group chose to focus on the norm: *Be present.* As Ms. Rivera presented her lesson plan, Mr. Holt leaned forward attentively, occasionally paraphrasing her points to ensure understanding and signal engagement.

After the team reviewed the lesson materials, Mr. Holt encouraged them to share "glows"—elements they found particularly strong. Mr. Vargas highlighted the interactive opening activity that engaged students in asking questions right from the start. Mr. Holt nodded, "That's a great way to spark curiosity. What other ways could we deepen questioning throughout the lesson?" Ms. Evans suggested adding question stems like "What if . . . ?" and "How might . . . ?" to scaffold students' inquiry.

Throughout the conversation, Mr. Holt ensured each voice was heard, prompting further exploration with questions like, "How can we help students think critically without overwhelming them?" This guided the group in refining practical adjustments aligned with their goal of fostering inquiry. As the meeting concluded, Mr. Holt summarized key ideas and asked Ms. Rivera how she planned to incorporate the feedback, ensuring she felt confident and supported. His thoughtful facilitation created a productive space where Ms. Rivera felt empowered to improve her approach, while others gained insights for their classrooms.

Riversedge High School: Bridging Gaps in Algebra With Collaborative Strategies

Welcome to Riversedge High School's 9th-grade PLC, where teachers are focused on addressing achievement gaps in algebra, particularly with multi-step equations. At the start of today's session, Ms. Jordan, the facilitator, introduced the Protocol for Analyzing Student Work, explaining that they would review samples from Mr. Lee's algebra class.

Mr. Lee shared student work samples ranging from proficient to struggling. He noted that many students tended to skip critical steps or apply incorrect operations when solving equations. Ms. Jordan encouraged the team to first examine the work independently and look for patterns before jumping to solutions. "What stands out to you as you look at these samples?" she asked, fostering an objective, evidence-based discussion.

Ms. Nguyen observed that students struggling with initial steps often faltered as they progressed through the problem. She suggested that foundational skills like isolating variables and understanding order of operations might need reinforcement. Ms. Jordan prompted further reflection, asking, "What strategies have you tried to support these foundational skills?" This led Mr. Lee to share his recent attempts with step-by-step minilessons.

The discussion deepened as Ms. Jordan guided a brainstorming session on ways to scaffold multistep problems. Ms. Nguyen described her use of visual aids to reinforce each step, while Ms. Carter suggested breaking problems into smaller segments. Ms. Jordan summarized these ideas, helping Mr. Lee identify a few targeted strategies to test in the coming weeks, including step-focused minilessons and visual supports.

CONCLUSION

In this chapter we explored essential functions and practices that effective PLC facilitators use to build a collaborative, growth-oriented environment. Through attentive listening, appreciative inquiry, strategic questioning, reflective dialogue, constructive feedback, and depersonalized language, facilitators can foster an atmosphere where rigorous and meaningful conversations take place. These practices bridge the gap between current teaching practices and a shared vision of improvement, embodying the reflective and inquiry-based approach at the heart of the VITAL framework.

To deepen your understanding and to help you refine your facilitation skills, we've included a self-assessment tool at the end of this chapter. Use this assessment to reflect on your current strengths and identify areas for further growth. By regularly revisiting this tool, you can monitor your progress, set specific goals for improvement, and align your practices with the strategies suggested above.

As we transition into Chapter 6, we will examine common challenges that facilitators may encounter and strategies for overcoming them. Understanding these potential obstacles will equip you to navigate difficulties effectively and sustain a productive, collaborative culture within your PLC.

PROMPTS FOR REFLECTION AND DISCUSSION

1. Review the core functions and key practices introduced in this chapter. How do the practices support the core functions?
2. Consider the practices described above. Which are you most comfortable with? Which provide the greatest opportunities for learning and growth?
3. Reflect on a recent PLC meeting you facilitated or participated in. Which of the core practices discussed in this chapter were most evident? Which practices could have been strengthened?
4. How do you currently balance the need for both appreciative inquiry and constructive feedback in your facilitation? What strategies might you use to improve in this area?
5. Consider the use of depersonalized language in your PLC. How does it impact the tone and productivity of your discussions? What steps

can you take to ensure that feedback remains focused on practices rather than individuals?

6. What are some specific examples of strategic questioning that have led to deeper discussions in your PLC? How can you expand your repertoire of strategic questions?
7. How can you create more opportunities for reflective dialogue within your PLC? What challenges might you face in doing so, and how could you address them?
8. What practices did you notice modeled in the case studies?

FACILITATION PRACTICES SELF-ASSESSMENT

Purpose

This self-assessment is designed to support reflection on core functions and practices of effective facilitation. By evaluating your practices, you can identify strengths and pinpoint areas for targeted growth that will enhance the quality of your facilitation and support meaningful collaboration in PLCs.

How to Use

For each prompt, rate yourself on a scale from 1 to 4, with 1 representing "Rarely" and 4 representing "Consistently." After each rating, reflect on specific actions or strategies to reinforce strengths or improve in areas where you rate yourself lower. Use this as part of your professional growth plan to support continuous improvement.

Self-Assessment Prompts

1. **Attentive Listening**
   - » How consistently do I engage in attentive listening to fully understand each participant's perspective, creating a space where all voices feel valued?
   - » Reflect on how you can enhance this function to better capture and respond to the nuances of team discussions.
2. **Appreciative Inquiry**
   - » How frequently do I apply appreciative inquiry techniques to highlight strengths and encourage a positive outlook in discussions?
   - » Think about a time when appreciative inquiry led to an "aha" moment for the group. How might you strengthen this core function in future meetings?
3. **Strategic Questioning**
   - » How effective are my questioning strategies in promoting deep reflection and guiding the team toward critical insights?
   - » Consider an instance where your questioning moved the team to deeper understanding. How could you further develop this function to maximize its impact?
4. **Promoting Reflective Dialogue**
   - » To what extent do I create an environment that supports reflective dialogue, helping team members critically analyze and improve their instructional practices?

   » Identify a specific approach that has worked well in fostering reflection and consider ways to expand on it to further support this core function.

5. **Encouraging Constructive Feedback**
   » How regularly do I encourage and model constructive feedback that focuses on growth and actionable improvement?
   » Reflect on the types of feedback shared in recent sessions. How can you help the team refine their feedback to align with their improvement goals?
6. **Depersonalizing Language**
   » How mindful am I of using language that keeps the focus on ideas, practices, and shared goals rather than individuals, to create a safe, constructive dialogue?
   » Consider how you can further practice depersonalizing language to enhance openness and reduce defensiveness in conversations.
7. **Goal-Setting and Alignment with PLC Objectives**
   » How effectively do I guide the team in setting specific, measurable goals that align with the larger objectives of our PLC and school improvement priorities?
   » Reflect on a time when clear goal-setting improved team focus and productivity. How might you strengthen this practice to ensure continuous alignment with PLC goals?
8. **Structured Process for Collaborative Analysis**
   » How consistently do I facilitate structured processes for analyzing data, student work, or teaching practices that promote collaborative problem solving?
   » Consider ways to enhance this process to ensure that each member contributes to and benefits from the collaborative analysis, leading to meaningful insights and improvements.
9. **Encouraging Shared Responsibility**
   » How well do I foster a sense of shared ownership and collective responsibility among team members for achieving our PLC goals?
   » Reflect on how you can strengthen this core function to empower each team member to take an active role in the team's success.

Next Steps

For any area where you rated yourself 2 or below, identify one concrete action you can take to strengthen this aspect of your facilitation. Consider sharing your reflections with a mentor or colleague to gain additional insights and build an actionable improvement plan.

CHAPTER 6

Overcoming Obstacles

Addressing Challenges in Facilitation

PRE-READING PROMPTS

1. What forces or factors do you think help drive and sustain effective facilitation and collaboration?
2. What forces or factors do you think hinder or restrain effective facilitation and collaboration?
3. Reflect on a time when a facilitation challenge significantly impacted your PLC's work or progress. How did you or the facilitator attempt to address or overcome that challenge?
4. For each of the statements below, indicate how true it is for you. (1 = not true at all. 4 = very true.)
    (a) I feel comfortable leading a PLC.
    (b) I know how to foster high levels of engagement in a PLC.
    (c) I know how to address resistance when it occurs in a PLC.
    (d) I know how to help my school leaders support our PLC.
    (e) I know how to make optimal use of time in a PLC.
    (f) I know how to strengthen the quality of feedback in a PLC.

INTRODUCTION

Building on the foundational beliefs and practices covered in the previous two chapters, this chapter highlights how a proactive, solutions-focused approach can empower facilitators to navigate the many complexities of leading PLCs effectively. Through our extensive work with teachers and PLC facilitators, we have seen firsthand the strengths, insights, and skills that effective PLC leaders can bring to the table, even as they confront difficult and recurring challenges.

When confronted with challenges, we have found that facilitators are often eager to learn how to address them. They want to deepen their confidence in guiding rigorous conversations with colleagues, to strengthen their capacity to engage all voices within their PLCs, and to enhance their strategies and techniques for constructively managing moments of resistance or pushback. Additionally, many facilitators demonstrate a strong desire to optimize the time available for PLC meetings, particularly when time is limited. Lastly, facilitators often ask how they can seek greater support from school leadership to sustain their team's collaborative work.

BUILDING CONFIDENCE IN FACILITATION

Facilitating high-stakes conversations with colleagues can be daunting, especially for those stepping into the role for the first time. This challenge often arises from factors such as unfamiliarity with the responsibilities of PLC facilitation, lack of experience, or concerns about navigating complex peer dynamics. However, stepping into a facilitator role presents a powerful opportunity to foster collaboration, growth, and shared leadership within PLCs. Done well, it is extremely fun and empowering. To assist with this, research shows that when facilitators have a clear understanding and definition of their role, they are more confident and effective in guiding discussions (Leithwood et al., 2004).

One essential strategy for building confidence with facilitating a PLC is to start with a clear definition of the facilitator's role and responsibilities. Collaborating with the PLC to clarify and document these expectations helps set a strong foundation. For example, PLC facilitators often play a lead role in guiding teams through protocols, gathering materials, and communicating with school leadership. It is also important to clarify what their role is not—such as an evaluator of instruction. Familiarizing oneself with tools like agenda templates and the protocols provided in Part III can bring structure to the role and enhance confidence. Practicing facilitation with peers, such as in a facilitator PLC, provides a safe space to refine skills and gain feedback. Finally, seeking mentorship from experienced facilitators can offer reassurance and a steady source of guidance, helping new facilitators grow into empowered teacher leaders.

CULTIVATING BUY-IN AND ENGAGEMENT

For facilitators, cultivating genuine buy-in and engagement among PLC members is key to maximizing the impact of collaboration. When teachers feel connected to the purpose of the PLC and see value in the process, they are more likely to contribute meaningfully and actively. Research highlights that psychological safety and trust are foundational to effective collaboration (Edmondson & Bransby, 2023). Without a sense of safety, teachers may hold back, resulting in surface-level discussions and limited progress.

Building engagement starts with establishing strong norms and agreements that emphasize trust, respect, and open communication. A protocol for setting these norms can be found in Part III of this book. Consistently reinforcing the PLC's vision and aligning its goals with schoolwide objectives can also drive motivation, as teachers see the broader impact of their work. Sharing success stories and specific examples of improvements driven by the PLC helps to highlight the tangible benefits of collaboration. Inviting teachers into decision-making and goal-setting processes can further strengthen commitment, fostering a sense of ownership that deepens engagement across the team.

Transforming Resistance Into Collaboration

At times, facilitators may encounter resistance within their PLCs. This can range from passive disengagement to active pushback. While this can initially seem discouraging, resistance often signals opportunities for deeper connection and growth. It is a natural response to change and can stem from uncertainty, fear of disruption, or misunderstanding of the PLC's goals. Embracing resistance, rather than avoiding it, can transform it into collaboration.

Addressing resistance begins with acknowledging it openly and identifying specific ways it appears. Berry's (2022) continuum of engagement, originally developed to assess student involvement, offers a valuable perspective on teacher engagement within PLCs. This continuum reminds us that participation is not binary but exists on a spectrum, where each level reflects varying degrees of investment and enthusiasm. By understanding this spectrum, facilitators can adopt a differentiated and nuanced approach to better support each team member's journey toward deeper and more impactful collaboration. Additionally, approaching resistance as an opportunity to understand and address underlying concerns allows facilitators to build trust and gradually guide colleagues toward a more engaged, collaborative stance. Table 6.1 lists some of the key behaviors associated with each level of the continuum.

As shown in the table, disengagement represents the lowest level of involvement, where participants may be physically present but mentally detached or disruptive, while deep engagement—"driving"—reflects a high level of enthusiasm, proactivity, and a commitment to continuous improvement. By using this continuum, facilitators can gain valuable insight into resistance as it manifests at various levels. For example, a teacher displaying passive resistance may be in the disengaged category, requiring strategies to reconnect them with the group's goals, while a teacher who complies without full enthusiasm may need support to move toward more meaningful participation. Understanding where a teacher falls on this continuum empowers facilitators to tailor their approach, viewing resistance not as a static obstacle but as a dynamic state that can shift toward deeper engagement with

Table 6.1. A Continuum of Participation in PLCs

Disengaged	Avoiding	Withdrawing	Participating	Investing	Driving
Distracting others. Disrupting conversations.	Looking for ways to skip meetings. Off-task behavior.	Being distracted. Physically separating from the group.	Fulfilling roles. Paying attention. Responding to questions.	Asking questions. Valuing the collaborative process.	Setting goals. Seeking feedback. Routine reflection.

Note: This table is based on Berry's (2022) research.

thoughtful support and strategies. Below we provide examples of common resistance behaviors that occur at the three lowest levels of engagement with suggestions for how a facilitator might respond.

Withdrawing

When a PLC member withdraws, it may involve sitting silently, avoiding eye contact, or opting out of activities that require collaboration, such as sharing a lesson or student work. Rather than interpreting withdrawal as a lack of interest, facilitators can view it as a cue that the teacher may need additional support or a new form of engagement. When withdrawal occurs, it is often challenging to understand the underlying reasons. A facilitator might approach the teacher privately, saying, "I've noticed you've been quieter lately. Your insights are always valuable to our discussions. How can we make the PLC meetings more relevant to what you're working on right now?" This approach respects the teacher's experience and seeks to understand their needs, opening a pathway to reengagement by making the PLC's work more aligned with their current focus. Once facilitators gain clarity on the reasons behind a colleague's withdrawal, potential solutions will often become clearer.

Avoiding

Avoidance behaviors in a PLC can include consistently missing meetings, arriving late, or redirecting conversations away from challenging topics. This behavior can sometimes appear passive-aggressive, such as frequently suggesting rescheduling or changing the subject when discussions require commitment. Avoidance may indicate that a teacher is struggling with the content or the group dynamics. Facilitators can address this by creating a safe space to discuss underlying concerns. For instance, a facilitator might say, "I've noticed it's been difficult to get everyone together lately. Is there something we could adjust about the timing or focus of our meetings to make them more beneficial for you?" This question fosters open dialogue and encourages the teacher to share their perspective, enabling the facilitator to make adjustments that promote consistent, engaged participation. As with withdrawal, a private, one-on-one conversation with the teacher can often make a significant difference.

Disengaging

Disengaging behaviors can vary widely, from frequent interruptions and off-topic comments to side conversations that detract from the main discussion. A PLC member may also openly challenge a facilitator's direction without offering constructive alternatives or make light of the group's progress. When disruption occurs, it can feel very off-putting. When it occurs, facilitators can use appreciative inquiry and an asset-oriented approach to mitigate the situation. Much like behavior management in the classroom, engaging in a power struggle is rarely productive.

Viewing disruption as a form of engagement can really help facilitators recognize that the disruptor may be seeking to assert influence or voice frustration. Sometimes facilitators can channel this energy constructively by acknowledging the teacher's desire to contribute and steering it toward positive dialogue. For example: "It sounds like you feel strongly about this topic, and that's valuable. Let's set aside some time to fully explore your ideas together." This response validates the teacher's input while setting clear expectations for how and when contributions should be made, refocusing their energy toward constructive outcomes. In addition to the above, here are some additional strategies for addressing disruptive behavior.

- *Revisit the Norms*: At the start of the PLC meeting, revisit team norms such as active listening, respecting differing opinions, and ensuring everyone has an opportunity to speak. Having these norms visible provides facilitators with a reference to gently guide discussions back on track when needed. For instance, if someone is interrupting, a facilitator might say, "Let's remember our norm about letting everyone finish their thoughts. This helps ensure all voices are heard and valued."
- *Gently Redirecting Off-Topic Comments*: If a member frequently veers off-topic, a gentle redirection can help. For example, "That's an interesting point. Let's hold onto it for later so we can stay focused on today's agenda." To help in situations like this, it can be useful to have a procedure for noting tangential ideas for future review through a community list or meeting minutes. For example, a "parking lot" on a piece of chart paper or in a running notes document in Google can help keep track of such ideas for future discussions.

- *Reframing Strong Opinions*: When someone holds a strong opinion, acknowledge it and reframe it in a way that benefits the group. For instance, "It sounds like you're passionate about this. How can we channel that into a solution that supports everyone's goals?"

Lastly, recognizing that resistance and disruptive behavior can make facilitation challenging, facilitators may benefit from additional support. A recommended strategy is for PLC facilitators within a school to meet regularly in a facilitator PLC to role-play challenging scenarios and build comfort in handling them. This practice not only strengthens skills but also fosters a supportive network. When all else fails, seeking support from school leaders can be a constructive step. The next section explores how facilitators can effectively approach school leaders for assistance.

SECURING PLC SUPPORT FROM LEADERSHIP

A strong partnership with school leaders can significantly enhance the impact of PLCs, sending a powerful message to teachers that collaborative work is valued and supported at all levels. When leaders actively support or participate in PLCs, it fosters a culture of shared responsibility and reinforces the priority of professional learning and growth. Research consistently highlights the role of supportive leadership as a key factor in successful PLCs (Hord et al., 2010). With leadership support, PLCs are more likely to secure the time, resources, and recognition they need to thrive.

Facilitators can encourage leader support by inviting school leaders to join PLC meetings or discussions, allowing them to see the PLC's goals in action and gain insight into the challenges teachers are working to address. This involvement helps leaders develop a deeper understanding of the PLC's value and increases their willingness to advocate for it. Working collaboratively with leaders to define roles and expectations within the PLC can also further align efforts and demonstrate a shared commitment to the PLC's success. Additionally, sharing data, success stories, and examples of how the PLC's work has positively impacted student outcomes can build a compelling case for sustained leadership support. Finally, when leaders participate regularly, they too may witness challenging behaviors from members when they occur and can work with the facilitator to mitigate them.

MAKING THE MOST OF LIMITED TIME

Finding time for meaningful collaboration within the constraints of a school's schedule is often a challenge for PLC facilitators. Limited time can lead to rushed meetings, surface-level discussions, and frustration among PLC members. Research underscores the importance of regular, sustained collaboration for effective PLCs (Vescio et al., 2008). Optimal PLC schedules generally include meetings once or twice a week, with 60 to 90 minutes per session, providing the time needed for deep reflection and continuous improvement in teaching practices and student outcomes (DuFour & Eaker, 1998; Vescio et al., 2008). This commitment needs to be sustained to see meaningful impact (Stoll et al., 2006).

When PLC time is limited, facilitators can work with school leaders to explore creative scheduling options, such as repurposing existing meeting times, implementing late-start or early-release days for collaboration, or integrating PLC activities into professional development days. *The School Leader's Guide to VITAL Collaboration* provides suggestions on how to do this. Additionally, spreading work across multiple meetings or focusing on high-impact goals can ensure that each session remains productive and focused, even with limited time. Establishing clear agendas aligned with the PLC's priorities can also help maximize each meeting's effectiveness.

Before seeking additional time for PLCs, it's essential to ensure that the time presently set aside for them is being used efficiently. In some schools, allotted PLC time is used for a variety of unrelated purposes, diluting its focus on instructional improvement. For PLCs to have their intended impact, they need dedicated time specifically for enhancing teaching practices. For instance, Common Planning Time (CPT) and PLCs serve different purposes and should be scheduled separately to preserve the focus of each. By refining how existing time is utilized, facilitators can often achieve more impactful collaboration without needing to increase the overall meeting frequency.

CASE STUDIES

Once again, let's revisit our three case study schools. Below, we provide examples of how facilitators in each of the schools successfully navigated some of the challenges described above. We encourage readers to name challenges and strategies for mitigating them when they occur. We also encourage readers to think about additional ways the facilitators could have proactively handled the situations described below.

Sunnyside Elementary: Building Confidence in Facilitation for 4th Grade

Continuing the school's emphasis on literacy development, the 4th-grade PLC at Sunnyside Elementary, led by literacy coach Ms. Garcia, focused on enhancing students' inferential reading skills. Over several months, Ms. Garcia guided the team through multiple Teaching and Learning Cycles (TLCs), concentrating on strategies like think-alouds and guided text connections. As they prepared to assess their progress, Ms. Garcia introduced the Protocol for Monitoring Progress of Teaching and Learning from Phase 3 of the VITAL framework to reflect on instructional shifts and their impact on student learning.

Sensing hesitation among team members, Ms. Garcia opened with a prompt, asking, "What are some noticeable patterns in how our students approach inferencing?" This allowed teachers to focus on observations instead of personal critiques, fostering a safe environment for sharing both successes and challenges.

When a few teachers drifted off-topic, Ms. Garcia used strategic questioning to guide the discussion back, asking, "How might our recent strategies influence these student behaviors?" and "What aspects of our instruction connect well with students?" Her questions helped the group refocus on instructional practices and their effects, steering them toward deeper analysis without disrupting the dialogue.

As they continued reviewing student work and assessment data, Ms. Garcia encouraged each teacher to highlight a specific strategy they'd tried and share evidence of its effect. For example, one teacher explained how modeling think-alouds led to more detailed student responses, prompting others to share similar experiences.

By the session's end, Ms. Garcia prompted a forward-looking discussion by asking, "What's one action each of us can take to support these gains over the next month?" The team members shared their commitments, with some refining questioning techniques and others planning additional scaffolds. This journey at Sunnyside Elementary illustrates how focused collaboration and student-centered engagement practices foster continuous professional growth and sustained literacy improvements.

Valley View Middle School: Strengthening Inquiry-Based Learning in 6th-Grade Science

At Valley View Middle School, Mr. Thompson, the Science Department Chair, led the 6th-grade PLC with a focus on enhancing inquiry-based learning in science. Over the past few months, the team engaged in multiple TLCs to foster student-led inquiry. While the teachers were making progress, some expressed uncertainty about the effectiveness of these techniques in deepening students' critical thinking skills.

To support reflective collaboration, Mr. Thompson introduced the Protocol for Discussing a Classroom Observation. He invited the group to observe Ms. Lee's lesson on ecosystems, where she structured an inquiry-based activity encouraging students to formulate and test their own hypotheses. The protocol offered a structured approach for the team to examine the lesson and share insights into the instructional shifts they had been practicing.

After the observation, the team reconvened, and Mr. Thompson opened with, "What stood out to you about how the students engaged with the inquiry activity?" This non-evaluative question allowed teachers to reflect on student behaviors and engagement without putting Ms. Lee on the spot. The team noted that while students eagerly shared their hypotheses, they struggled to connect findings to broader ecological principles.

When the conversation began shifting to broader behavioral challenges, Mr. Thompson refocused the group by asking, "How did the lesson structure support or hinder students' exploration of the topic?" This brought the team back to instructional goals and encouraged critical thinking about specific aspects of Ms. Lee's approach.

During the reflection, Ms. Rivera shared her concern that students seemed hesitant to take risks with their hypotheses, which limited deeper inquiry. Recognizing this as a shared challenge, Mr. Thompson facilitated a collaborative problem-solving session, asking, "What strategies have we tried to encourage students to feel safe making predictions or taking risks?" This prompted teachers to share ideas for fostering a supportive inquiry environment, such as modeling "safe" mistakes and framing incorrect answers as learning opportunities.

As the conversation concluded, Mr. Thompson guided the team to identify specific adjustments to try in upcoming lessons. To reinforce shared learning, he asked, "What's one takeaway from today's discussion that you'd like to apply in your own classroom?" Each teacher shared a practical insight, from adding scaffolding to open-ended tasks to creating prompts that help students connect findings to broader scientific concepts.

Riversedge High School: Aligning Instructional Goals in 10th-Grade Algebra

Despite shared objectives, differing opinions and disruptive behaviors sometimes create obstacles in PLC meetings. Welcome to Riversedge High School's 10th-grade PLC, where teachers face the challenge of aligning instructional goals to close achievement gaps in algebra. As part of Phase 1 of VITAL Collaboration, Ms. Jordan led the team in setting a focused teaching improvement goal to drive measurable results.

At the start of the meeting, Ms. Jordan introduced the Protocol for Developing Teaching Improvement Goals, encouraging the team to reflect on recent assessment data. Early in the session, one teacher expressed frustration with the protocol's structure, while another voiced skepticism about setting measurable goals. Recognizing the potential disruption, Ms. Jordan responded calmly, acknowledging their concerns without deviating from the process. She reminded the team, "This protocol helps us identify a goal grounded in our students' needs and ensures each of us contributes to achieving it."

To address the disruptions, Ms. Jordan restated the norms and invited the team to reaffirm their commitment to respectful listening and collaborative problem-solving. As the session continued, Ms. Jordan guided the team in examining specific gaps in student understanding of algebraic concepts. She encouraged each teacher to contribute one observation, creating a space for all voices.

Gradually, the team coalesced around a goal: to increase students' mastery of multistep equations through consistent use of scaffolded problem-solving techniques. Ms. Jordan facilitated a brief reflection, asking, "What's one step we can each take to incorporate this focus into our classrooms?" Each teacher left with a specific action plan, including visual aids and targeted questioning strategies to support students' mastery of multistep processes.

CONCLUSION

In Chapters 4 through 6, we've explored the foundational beliefs, essential practices, and common challenges that effective PLC facilitators encounter. Chapter 4 set the stage by defining the attributes and beliefs that underpin effective facilitation, emphasizing the importance of a shared vision, psychological safety, and the facilitator's role as both a leader and learner. Chapter 4 also illustrated how these beliefs translate into the various roles a facilitator must fulfill, from Vision Keeper to Instructional Leader, each contributing to a collaborative environment focused on growth.

In Chapter 5, we dove into the core practices and techniques that successful facilitators use to guide productive discussions and promote reflective dialogue. These included skills like attentive listening, strategic questioning, and appreciative inquiry, all of which enable facilitators to foster a culture of continuous improvement and open communication. These are essential for laying the groundwork for meaningful collaboration. The techniques shared in Chapter 5 are instrumental in building a supportive PLC where members feel valued and motivated to engage deeply in the collaborative process.

Finally, in Chapter 6 we explored challenges facilitators often face, such as managing resistance, securing leadership support, and optimizing limited time. By reframing these challenges as opportunities, facilitators can use targeted strategies to strengthen team dynamics, nurture buy-in, and advocate for the time and resources necessary to achieve PLC goals. This chapter provided practical solutions that enable facilitators to navigate obstacles with resilience and adaptability, reinforcing the importance of a proactive, asset-oriented approach.

Having gained a solid foundation of beliefs, practices, and problem-solving strategies, facilitators are now prepared to dive into the structured protocols that bring these concepts to life. In Part III, we introduce a suite of protocols designed to guide facilitators through each phase of the VITAL Collaboration framework. These protocols offer a roadmap for implementing the skills and concepts discussed in Part II and provide practical steps that facilitators can use to lead their teams through each stage of collaboration, from setting goals to celebrating achievements. Equipped with these tools, facilitators will be empowered to turn the theory of effective facilitation into impactful practice, driving sustained improvement in teaching and learning.

PROMPTS FOR FURTHER REFLECTION AND DISCUSSION

- What challenges and strategies shared in this chapter were you most familiar with? Why?
- Reflect on a time when you successfully navigated a facilitation challenge in your PLC. What strategies did you use? How did these compare to those shared above? What was the outcome?
- How might you apply the suggestions in this chapter to improve your current PLC's effectiveness?
- What can you do to ensure that your school leaders remain supportive of your PLC's work?
- Consider the following scenarios. How would you apply the strategies and techniques shared in this chapter to resolve the situation?
    - *Scenario 1: Transforming Resistance Into Engagement.* In your PLC, one of the team members frequently expresses frustration with the new strategies the group discusses. They often vocalize that their current methods are sufficient and seem hesitant to embrace changes. During meetings, they occasionally cross their arms or look away, visibly disengaged when new ideas are introduced. This attitude sometimes influences others, creating a subtle undercurrent of resistance. Reflecting on the techniques in this chapter, consider how you might foster a more open mindset in this colleague. What steps would you take to validate their experiences while encouraging them to consider alternative approaches? How might you use appreciative inquiry or reflective questioning to help them see the potential benefits of trying something new?
    - *Scenario 2: Building Confidence as a New Facilitator.* You have recently taken on the role of PLC facilitator. Although you bring a fresh perspective and enthusiasm, you're aware that some of your colleagues have more experience in the classroom.

During meetings, a few team members subtly challenge your suggestions, which at times makes you second-guess your approach. You want to establish credibility and foster a trusting, collaborative environment, but you're unsure of how best to do so. Drawing on strategies from this chapter, think about how you can use active listening, strategic questioning, and perhaps even small successes to build your confidence and that of the group. How can you create a space where everyone feels valued, including yourself, and where team members are more open to following your facilitation?

» *Scenario 3: Managing Time Constraints in PLC Meetings.* Your PLC has ambitious goals, but each session feels rushed due to limited meeting time. Important discussions often run long, leaving key items on the agenda unaddressed. Team members leave the meetings feeling both overwhelmed and that essential topics are continually postponed. To ensure productivity and meet your objectives, you need to apply time management techniques effectively. Reflecting on this chapter's insights, consider how you might structure the agenda to maximize efficiency without sacrificing meaningful conversation. How might you balance setting boundaries on certain topics while allowing enough time for team members to share their insights? What strategies could you use to help the team prioritize their goals and stay on track?
» *Scenario 4: Encouraging Constructive Feedback Without Personal Critique.* In a recent PLC session focused on analyzing a lesson observation, feedback from some team members became personal rather than professional, leading to defensive responses. For example, one team member commented directly on a peer's teaching style rather than on specific practices or outcomes. As a result, the conversation turned tense, and the group did not reach a constructive discussion about how to improve instruction. To create a more supportive and objective feedback culture, reflect on how you might depersonalize the language used in these sessions. Drawing on this chapter, think about how you could encourage team members to focus on specific practices and observable impacts on student learning. How could you model the language and approach you hope to see, helping the team provide feedback in a way that feels constructive and forward-focused?

Part III

THE VITAL FACILITATOR'S TOOLBOX

Welcome to Part III of this Teacher's Guide. Part III gives facilitators a comprehensive set of protocols that are at the heart of the VITAL Collaboration framework. These protocols guide teams through structured processes, allowing them to work systematically through all four phases of VITAL Collaboration: preparing, engaging in teaching and learning cycles, studying impact, and sharing learning. In this part, you will find practical tools designed to help facilitators keep their PLCs focused, productive, and aligned with the overarching goals of improving teaching and learning.

Chapter 7, "VITAL Protocols: Building Blocks for Structured Collaboration," provides an overview of how most of the VITAL protocols are designed. Protocols, even at their best, offer only a structured framework to help guide conversations. They are not intended to be scripts that facilitators follow blindly. Just as a river guide leading paddlers down the river has a mental map of the rapids and knows the boat, but needs to adjust to circumstances of weather and water along the way, so the facilitator implementing the protocols below must react and improvise. In short, knowing the architecture and design features of the protocols helps facilitators navigate through the complexity that comes with leading conversations with peers.

PROTOCOLS FOR PHASE 1: PREPARING TO ENGAGE IN TEACHING AND LEARNING CYCLES

Chapter 8, "A Protocol for Establishing PLC Norms," lays the foundation for effective collaboration by helping teams create norms that guide their interactions. Establishing clear expectations for behavior and communication sets a positive tone for the work ahead, ensuring that all members feel valued and heard. This protocol is essential for building trust and creating a culture of respect, which are key to the success of VITAL Collaboration.

Chapter 9, "A Protocol for Setting Student Learning Goals," guides facilitators in leading teams to analyze data and set specific, measurable goals. This process provides a clear focus for the team's efforts and ensures that their work is aligned with student learning needs. By grounding their collaboration in data, teams can identify areas for improvement, set targets, and track progress, setting the stage for the teaching and learning cycles that follow.

Chapter 10, "A Protocol for Developing Teaching Improvement Goals," provides a process for teachers to set targeted, research-based teaching improvement goals. This protocol helps align individual practices with the team's student learning goals, creating coherence across the PLC's work. By focusing on instructional practices that directly impact student outcomes, this protocol ensures that the collaborative process is both purposeful and impactful.

PROTOCOLS FOR PHASE 2: ENGAGING IN TEACHING AND LEARNING CYCLES

Chapter 11, "A Protocol for Analyzing Standards," focuses on helping teams unpack and analyze the standards they aim to teach. By clarifying the expectations of these standards, teachers can develop a shared understanding of what students need to learn and how best to support their progress. This protocol serves as a critical step in refining lesson planning and assessment strategies, supporting deeper alignment with student learning goals.

Chapter 12, "A Protocol for Tuning a Lesson," guides teams in refining lessons through structured feedback and collaborative discussion. By presenting and tuning lessons before they are taught, teachers can anticipate challenges, receive input, and make adjustments to maximize student engagement and learning. This protocol exemplifies the reflective practice at the heart of VITAL Collaboration, promoting a cycle of continuous improvement.

Chapter 13, "A Protocol for Discussing a Classroom Observation," provides guidance on observing instruction in a classroom and then discussing it during the PLC. This protocol focuses on analyzing a teacher's instruction in action as they apply strategies and techniques aligned to the teaching improvement goal.

Chapter 14, "A Protocol for Analyzing Student Work," offers a step-by-step process for examining student work to assess the impact of instruction and identify next steps. By analyzing student artifacts, teams can evaluate the effectiveness of their teaching strategies and make informed adjustments to their practice. This protocol embodies the data-driven, reflective nature of VITAL Collaboration, ensuring that the work of the PLC is grounded in student outcomes.

PROTOCOLS FOR PHASES 3 AND 4: STUDYING IMPACT AND SHARING LEARNING

Chapter 15, "A Protocol for Monitoring Progress of Teaching and Learning," provides a framework for teams to assess their progress toward established goals. By revisiting and reviewing both student learning and teaching improvement goals, teams can measure their impact, celebrate successes, and identify areas for further growth. This protocol supports a culture of accountability and continuous learning within the PLC.

Chapter 16, "A Protocol for Sharing and Celebrating Learning," emphasizes the importance of reflecting on and sharing the results of collaborative efforts. By highlighting successes and discussing challenges, teams can reinforce their commitment to improvement and foster a sense of collective achievement. This protocol helps to build a community of practice, extending the benefits of VITAL Collaboration beyond individual teams to the wider school community.

By the end of Part III, facilitators will be equipped with a suite of protocols to guide their teams through each phase of VITAL Collaboration. These tools are designed to structure the collaborative work, keeping it focused, data-driven, and aligned with the goals of improving teaching and learning.

CHAPTER 7

VITAL Protocols

Building Blocks for Structured Collaboration

PRE-READING PROMPTS

- Think about protocols your PLC has used in the past. How effective were they in guiding your discussions and decision-making? What elements of those protocols worked well, and what aspects could be improved?
- Consider the specific goals your PLC aims to achieve. How might a well-designed protocol help you stay focused on these goals during meetings? What features do you believe are essential for a protocol to be effective in your context?
- Every PLC has unique needs based on its members and goals. How can you ensure that the protocols you use are flexible and adaptable to meet these needs? Reflect on any past experiences where a protocol either supported or hindered your collaborative efforts.
- As you read this chapter, think about what you hope to learn regarding the construction of protocols. Are there specific challenges or opportunities in your current PLC that you think a well-crafted protocol could address?

INTRODUCTION

Given the intricate nature of protocols as compared to simpler tools, this chapter provides an overview of the key features that inform the design and rationale of the VITAL Collaboration protocols introduced in the chapters that follow. Understanding their design and intent is crucial for facilitators to implement them as intended and to create the space for meaningful collaboration and growth. These protocols are specifically designed to strengthen both individual and collective teacher efficacy. Through the structured conversations the protocols are designed to foster, PLC leaders can work with their teams to set common goals, share insights, and provide constructive feedback, ultimately leading to improved teaching practices and better educational outcomes for students. By exploring the rationale behind these protocols, readers should gain valuable insights into enhancing their collaborative discussions. This understanding equips facilitators to guide discussions effectively, implement the protocols with fidelity, and adapt them as needed without compromising their core principles. Ultimately, this chapter aims to empower educators to fully utilize the VITAL protocols and maximize their impact.

KEY COMPONENTS

Although each of the VITAL Collaboration protocols focuses on enhancing a specific aspect of teaching practice, they share many common features and components. First, each protocol chapter includes an overview of the protocol showcased in the chapter with guidance for using it effectively. The overview begins by explaining the purpose of the protocol and how long it typically takes to complete it, as well as materials and suggestions to help facilitators prepare for implementing it. Each overview also describes some challenges that may arise when using the protocol with suggestions on how to navigate through these. Finally, each protocol concludes with an outline of the steps to follow.

For the most part, the VITAL protocols share a common framework of five stages: *organize, review, discuss, evaluate,* and *recap* (ORDER). This framework provides an invisible architecture that helps facilitators understand the general flow and progression most protocols need to take and that are needed to foster conversations that are robust and rigorous enough to transform professional practice.

The acronym ORDER aids facilitators in recalling both the design and intent of the VITAL protocols. Most protocols begin with what we often refer to as table-setting—making sure everything is organized and in order. Since most protocols require some form of analysis, the next stage is reviewing materials so that participants have time to analyze and process any information being put on the table. After participants have had time to review materials, they need to be given time to discuss their thinking, ask questions, and/or provide feedback. Once a robust discussion has taken place, it is important for PLC members to reflect on or evaluate how the discussion went. Most protocols then end with an attempt to recap or bring closure that prepares members for the next PLC. Understanding each stage's purpose enables facilitators to judge when a collaborative team is prepared to advance to the next stage. A detailed description of these stages is provided below. Each protocol is different, and not all steps appear in all protocols. However, most appear across most of them.

STAGE 1: ORGANIZE

A described throughout this book, the mission of VITAL Collaboration is to help schools create a replicable approach to collaboration that transforms teaching practice during every protocol-driven conversation with the intended impact of improving collective teacher efficacy. To achieve this vision, it is necessary to organize each discussion effectively. Below are common action steps that help facilitators start on the right foot when facilitating a protocol. These include setting roles, revisiting norms, clarifying the purpose, presenting any materials, and clarifying initial understanding.

Setting Roles

Various roles need to be fulfilled during a protocol-driven conversation. At the outset, it is important for every team member to have a clear understanding of their role and responsibilities. Common roles include:

- **Facilitator**: Guides the conversation, ensuring it meets the team's needs and achieves the intended outcome.
- **Presenter**: Shares an artifact of their teaching work, describes it, answers clarifying questions, and shares learning goals.
- **Timekeeper**: Monitors time and informs the group when a specific step is almost over.
- **Note-taker**: Captures essential notes, particularly ideas and actions generated from discussions and reflections.
- **Process Observer**: Pays attention to the discussion and looks for what is working, as well as where and how there may be opportunities to improve future conversations.

Revisiting Norms

Every PLC should have well-established norms and working agreements. These should be frequently revisited to ensure they remain relevant and effective. Neglecting this step can lead to challenges that require norms to be resurfaced, which can feel punitive if they were previously ignored. During Phase 1 of VITAL Collaboration, PLCs are encouraged to establish or reset their norms.

Clarifying the Purpose

Clarifying the purpose of the meeting at the outset is very important. This often involves reminding the team of the protocol they are using, why they are using it, and what they hope to accomplish by the end of the meeting.

Presenting Materials

Presenting materials for peer consideration and review is often key during the organizing stage. This is where teachers make their work visible and transparent to their colleagues. The presenter introduces and provides an overview of what the team will be reviewing and discussing, ensuring everyone understands the presented materials.

Clarifying Initial Understanding

After materials are presented, team members are asked if they have clarifying questions to make sure they achieve a common understanding of what has been presented. These questions are typically straightforward and should be able to be answered quickly.

Confirming the Focus for Learning

A final step in the organizing stage is often confirming or establishing the focus for learning. This is particularly true for protocols focused on generating feedback. When feedback is the focus for the protocol, the person or people receiving feedback should explain what kind of feedback they would like. As discussed earlier, remember that receiving feedback can feel threatening. Therefore, it is important for permission to be given. When a person gives permission for others to provide feedback, and when they help direct the nature and focus of the feedback, they will in turn feel more empowered. In addition, this helps create a culture where feedback is seen as a gift rather than as a threat (Forsythe & Johnson, 2017: Ryan & Deci, 2022) and, by making a potentially difficult conversation easier, ensures the team can gain a clear understanding of the learning goals or desired takeaways from the discussion.

STAGE 2: REVIEW

Once the table is set and everything is in order, team members should independently review and analyze any materials that have been presented. This stage provides time for silent review and note-taking in preparation for the discussion. Facilitators should make sure that the time provided for review should be commensurate with the complexity of material shared and take into consideration how familiar members are with what has been shared. Encouraging a growth mindset and providing structured templates for note-taking can help team members stay focused on learning and growth as they review and process.

Many of the VITAL protocols also encourage team members to provide feedback as a result of their review of materials. Feedback is a critical component of the VITAL Collaboration protocols, designed to support growth and development within teaching practices. When feedback is expected, facilitators should guide team members in organizing their feedback effectively. We recommend three simple frameworks for structuring feedback: Glows and Grows; Praise, Probe, Polish; and the GROW framework. Each framework offers a unique approach to fostering constructive and supportive discussions within your team. We encourage PLCs to use any of these.

Glows and Grows

The Glows and Grows framework provides a straightforward way to structure feedback. Glows are positive affirmations that highlight what is working well, what is appreciated, or what should be celebrated. This type of feedback can take the form of praise, recognition, or affirmations that reinforce effective practices. On the other hand, Grows are constructive suggestions aimed at helping a colleague improve and strengthen their teaching practice. This feedback focuses on areas for growth and offers specific ideas for enhancement.

Praise, Probe, Polish

The Praise, Probe, Polish framework builds upon Glows and Grows by adding an additional dimension focused on inquiry. This approach not only celebrates strengths, but it also encourages critical thinking and reflection. Below is a brief overview of each component.

Praise. Similar to Glows, this is where positive feedback is given. Praise highlights what is successful or commendable in the data, teaching practice, or artifact being discussed.

Probe. This element introduces questions aimed at deeper reflection. Probing questions are designed to help the recipient think critically about their practice, explore different perspectives, and consider potential improvements. Compared to clarifying questions, which should elicit quick responses, probing questions should be open-ended and thought-provoking, encouraging the recipient to engage in reflective dialogue.

Polish. In this step, constructive feedback is offered to refine and enhance practice. This is where suggestions are made to improve or "polish" aspects of the teaching approach, lesson plan, or other educational artifacts under discussion. The goal is to provide actionable, supportive advice that helps colleagues advance their skills and effectiveness.

The GROW Framework

The GROW framework provides an even more comprehensive approach to organizing feedback by introducing another element to that of the Praise, Probe, Polish framework: working together. This fourth element is particularly helpful if a facilitator wishes to encourage PLC members to identify when or how feedback might apply to all members of the team, thus encouraging collective improvements in teaching. This framework is particularly effective in fostering a balanced and holistic discussion within teams and helps remind teams that the purpose of their work is to improve collective teacher efficacy. Once again we summarize each element below. Notice the overlap with the other frameworks.

Give Praise. Begin feedback by acknowledging what works well. Recognizing strengths sets a positive tone and reinforces the collaborative spirit of the team. Praise should be specific, highlighting what is effective and why it is successful.

Raise Probing Questions. As mentioned above, probing questions are a powerful tool for encouraging deep reflection. These questions should be framed to inspire recipients to think about their practice in new and innovative ways, challenging them to explore alternative approaches or consider different perspectives.

Offer Suggestions. As already discussed, constructive suggestions are essential for guiding improvement. This type of feedback should be clear, specific, and actionable, providing direct advice on how to enhance teaching practices. As always, facilitators should encourage colleagues to frame suggestions positively and use depersonalized language.

Work Together. Finally, feedback can sometimes suggest collective action. Facilitators should encourage team members to identify opportunities for groupwide improvements that can enhance collective efficacy. For example, during a lesson tuning protocol, if a suggestion is made for one teacher to create a graphic organizer, the team might discuss how to implement this tool across multiple classrooms and share their results in a future meeting. This collaborative approach reinforces the power of shared learning and collective growth within the team.

By employing any of these frameworks, facilitators can ensure that feedback within VITAL protocols is organized, constructive, and geared toward fostering both individual and collective improvement. This structured approach to feedback not only enhances the quality of discussions but also strengthens the overall impact of the collaborative process.

STAGE 3: DISCUSS

After the team has had time to review materials and organize any feedback, the team shifts to discussing. During the Discuss stage, PLC members share their findings and discuss them with each other. At this time, facilitators may need to reemphasize the focus for learning, conduct a time check, and/or determine how collaborators will share their insights. Prioritizing listening and ensuring everyone has a chance to share before diving into deep discussion are crucial for a balanced and productive conversation. It is also important to make sure that discussions begin with positive affirmations and/or a recognition of assets. It is not uncommon for team members to begin discussions by wanting to talk about what appears to be going wrong, what could be improved, or what is frustrating them. Facilitators must be aware of this and make sure to begin with the positive. It is often at this stage of a protocol that PLC members may shift to using deficit-oriented or personalized language.

STAGE 4: EVALUATE

In this stage of a VITAL protocol, teams take time to reflect on the discussion and share takeaways. Facilitators should often begin this stage by restating the focus for learning and/or the purpose of the protocol to help orient reflections and encourage all team members to share their insights.

In addition to sharing insights and takeaways, the evaluation stage is also an opportunity to metacognitively reflect on the process and to suggest potential adjustments to norms, roles, or the protocol itself. This is the moment when anyone serving as a process observer would share their observations.

STAGE 5: RECAP

The final stage of many VITAL protocols involves bringing the process to closure and preparing for the next conversation. Facilitators should determine the next protocol to be used, if a presenter will be needed, clarify the timing of the next meeting, and confirm any preparatory actions required. Recapping helps to summarize the key points and ensures that all participants are clear on the outcomes and next steps.

USING THE VITAL PROTOCOLS

As you prepare to delve into the protocols that follow, it is helpful to think of them as a map for planning PLC meetings to guide your team through the four phases of VITAL Collaboration. Each phase has specific goals and activities, and the protocols provide a structure to facilitate meaningful conversations and decision-making. Many PLCs move through all four phases in a semester. Some take a year. Below is a general overview of the flow.

Phase 1: Preparing to Engage in Teaching and Learning Cycles

The protocols in Phase 1 focus on laying the foundation for effective collaboration. This includes establishing norms, reviewing data, and setting clear learning goals for students and teachers. For example, the *Protocol for Establishing PLC Norms* is designed to help teams create a shared understanding of how they will work together. This protocol can be used during the first few meetings to establish a safe and productive collaborative environment. By clarifying expectations, team members can engage in open and honest dialogue throughout the year.

Once norms are in place, the *Protocol for Setting Student Learning Goals* guides the team through a series of discussions centered on student data. During these meetings, the team identifies key areas of student need and sets specific, measurable goals. For instance, if the data reveals a gap in student writing skills, the team might set a goal to improve students' use of evidence in their writing. This goal-setting process provides focus for the subsequent teaching and learning cycles.

After PLCs set student learning goals, it is time to establish a *teaching improvement goal* using the protocol with the same name. The purpose of the teaching improvement protocol is to identify an element of instructional practice for the team to improve that, if achieved, will help produce the desired student learning outcome (see the Theory of Improvement in Chapter 2). For example, a team that wants to improve listening comprehension for their 1st-grade students may set a goal to enhance how they teach students to construct images as they listen to a teacher read. Once a PLC has a teaching improvement goal established, it is time to move into Phase. 2.

Phase 2: Engaging in Teaching and Learning Cycles

In Phase 2, the PLC moves into the core of VITAL Collaboration: Teaching and Learning Cycles (TLCs). A TLC consists of four inquiry-based conversations: analyzing standards, tuning a lesson, observing and discussing instruction, and analyzing student work. The protocols used in this phase help structure these activities and keep the focus on improving instructional practice.

The *Protocol for Analyzing Standards* provides a structured approach for reviewing standards that will be the focus of a lesson that is going to be tuned. Often, the standards lessons are designed to address are complicated and ambiguous. It is essential that teachers have a clear and common understanding of what a focus standard is expecting students to be able to do and what they need to know in order to do it. This analysis often takes a full meeting, and the protocol helps teacher achieve this understanding.

The *Lesson Tuning Protocol* is at the heart of the teaching and learning cycle. In this step, one team member presents a lesson they plan to teach, highlighting areas where they would like feedback. The team then provides input, offering suggestions and refining the lesson to align with the team's goals. After tuning, the lesson is taught and may be observed by other team members, either in real time or via video. This observation focuses on gathering detailed insights into how the lesson unfolds and how students respond.

Once the lesson has been taught, the team meets to debrief the lesson that they observed. Using the *Protocol for Discussing a Classroom Observation*, a PLC facilitator encourages the team to share what they noticed during the instruction, focusing on what went well and where there are opportunities to enhance teaching and learning.

Finally, the *Protocol for Analyzing Student Work* brings the TLC to a close. PLCs use this protocol to examine the work produced by students during the lesson that was tuned and/or observed. This protocol guides the team in discussing the successes and challenges observed, helping them identify adjustments for future instruction. For example, the team might notice that students struggled with providing evidence in their writing, prompting a discussion on how to modify future lessons to address this gap.

By repeating this cycle of analyzing standards, tuning lessons, observing instruction, and reviewing student work, teams iteratively refine their practices and directly address students' evolving needs, bringing them ever closer to achieving their teaching improvement goal.

Phase 3: Studying Impact

After completing several teaching and learning cycles, it is crucial for teams to study the outcomes of their efforts. Phase 3 involves using a protocol that focuses on gathering and analyzing new data to measure progress against the goals set in Phase 1. *The Protocol for Monitoring Progress of Teaching and Learning* provides structure for this discussion. This protocol guides the team through a series of questions to assess whether the changes in teaching practices have led to measurable improvements in student learning. For example, if the initial goal was to improve students' use of evidence in writing, the team would analyze new writing samples to see if students are now incorporating evidence more effectively. This phase typically involves fewer meetings but is strategically placed throughout the year to ensure ongoing assessment and reflection.

Phase 4: Sharing and Celebrating Learning

The final phase of VITAL Collaboration focuses on sharing and celebrating learning. Using the *Protocol for Sharing and Celebrating Learning*, teams are encouraged to reflect on, share, and celebrate their growth and progress. This protocol not only provides an opportunity for teams to document their journey and successes but also to share their learning with others in the school community. For example, at the end of a semester, the team might use this protocol to present their learning journey to colleagues, highlighting key achievements and insights gained from the process. This sharing fosters a culture of transparency, accountability, and collective improvement. Celebrating successes helps to reinforce the value of collaboration and sets a positive tone for future cycles of VITAL Collaboration.

By mapping out PLC meetings aligned with the four phases of VITAL Collaboration and integrating the relevant protocols, your team can maintain a clear focus and structure throughout the year. This approach supports continuous improvement and ensures that collaboration remains purposeful and directly tied to enhancing student learning outcomes. As you explore the protocols that follow, consider how they can guide your team's yearlong journey of collaborative learning and improvement.

CONCLUSION

Understanding the anatomy of a VITAL protocol and how they are designed to work in concert is essential for facilitating high-quality collaboration in your PLCs. By breaking down the process into five stages, each with specific activities and goals, these protocols provide a clear structure for guiding productive discussions and decision-making. However, the true power of these protocols lies in their use as a map for scheduling and guiding your team through the four phases of VITAL Collaboration over the course of the school year.

As you prepare to explore the protocols in the chapters that follow, consider how they can support your team in planning a yearlong journey of collaborative learning and growth. The structure they provide helps to maintain focus, align efforts with student learning goals, and make collaboration a purposeful, impactful driver of improvement in your school. By using the protocols as a guide for scheduling your PLC meetings, you ensure that each stage of VITAL Collaboration is addressed, setting your team up for success in achieving meaningful, student-centered outcomes.

PROMPTS FOR REFLECTION AND DISCUSSION

- Reflect on the protocols currently in use within your PLC. Based on what you've learned, how might you redesign these protocols to better align with your collaborative goals? What specific changes could enhance their effectiveness?
- Consider the process of constructing a new protocol for your PLC. What steps will you take to ensure that this protocol is both rigorous

and adaptable? How will you involve your team in the design process to ensure it meets their needs?

- How can you ensure that the protocols you are using in your PLC are closely aligned with your PLC's objectives? Discuss how a protocol might help maintain focus on specific goals, such as improving student outcomes or enhancing teaching practices.
- Once a new protocol is in place, how can you assess its effectiveness? What feedback mechanisms can you incorporate to refine the protocol over time, ensuring it remains relevant and effective?
- Think about how the consistent use of well-designed protocols could influence the culture of collaboration in your PLC. How can protocols help foster a more structured, goal-oriented approach to your meetings and discussions?

CHAPTER 8

A Protocol for Establishing PLC Norms

INTRODUCTION

Establishing norms within a PLC is a foundational step during Phase 1 of VITAL Collaboration, a step that supports productive collaboration and sets a tone and culture of trust, respect, and accountability. Norms clarify expectations for behavior, and they can significantly influence how members interact, communicate, and engage in their collaborative work (Carmi et al., 2022; Lee et al., 2024). Through setting norms, PLCs build a shared understanding that enhances cohesion and creates a structure to help the team achieve its goals for improvement. This chapter introduces a structured protocol for establishing or revisiting norms, ensuring that all members are aligned in their expectations for collaboration.

PURPOSE

The purpose of *Protocol for Establishing PLC Norms* is to create a unified approach to collaboration within the PLC. Setting norms helps prevent misunderstandings, keeps discussions on track, and upholds a respectful and productive environment. By defining clear behavioral expectations, norms help to support a consistent, focused team dynamic and allow for smoother, more effective communication in pursuit of PLC goals.

SUGGESTED TIME

This protocol generally requires 60 to 90 minutes. This amount of time is needed for meaningful discussion, reflection, and consensus-building.

MATERIALS

- The *Protocol for Establishing PLC Norms*
- Chart paper or whiteboard
- Markers or pens
- Sticky notes
- A template for documenting the final norms

PREPARATION

Prior to engaging in the protocol, the PLC facilitator should review any existing norms or working agreements previously used in the group or school. If these do not exist, the facilitator can prepare examples to spark discussion. A list of norms we commonly encounter is provided below. Participants may also be encouraged to reflect in advance on past experiences in collaborative settings to identify both positive and challenging behaviors that could inform a new or revised set of group norms.

PROCESS OVERVIEW

The section below provides facilitators with a walk-through of the protocol with guidance for each step. Each step is designed to ensure participants feel heard, valued, and aligned in their expectations for collaborative behavior. This overview should be reviewed before beginning the protocol to help facilitators prepare to lead each part of the session effectively.

Step 1: Establish Roles and Purpose

To start, the facilitator begins by clarifying participant roles for the session. For this protocol the needed roles are a facilitator, timekeeper, and note-taker. Begin with a brief explanation of the purpose of establishing norms and how they will support the group's collaborative goals. This sets a professional tone, signaling the importance of everyone's participation in building a positive PLC culture.

Step 2: Reflect on Past Practices

Next, the facilitator invites participants to reflect on their past experiences in previous PLCs or other collaborative settings. Ask them to consider what behaviors or practices have contributed to productive or unproductive meetings. When doing so, ask that they not include names and just keep the information to behaviors they have experienced. Give the group a few minutes to jot down their thoughts on sticky notes or paper. This step creates an opportunity for individuals to draw from real experiences and encourages them to think critically about what they need to feel supported in their PLC.

Step 3: Review Existing or Baseline Norms

If your team or school has existing norms, share these with the group as a starting point. If needed, explain each norm briefly and invite participants to ask questions or share reflections. This allows the team to work from a baseline and determine whether these norms still align with their current goals or need adjustments. For groups without preexisting norms, Table 8.1 lists norms we encourage teams to consider as a starting point. While this list includes more norms than we typically recommend teams use, they comprise the most common ones we have come across. Some of these norms are also adapted from the "seven norms of collaboration" developed by Garmston and Wellman (2016).

Step 4: Crosswalk Norms With Reflections

Facilitate a discussion that connects the shared reflections with any existing norms or guidelines. As participants identify connections, they begin to see where current norms already align with productive behaviors or where gaps might exist. For example, in Step 2, someone may have commented that a behavior that could hinder a team meeting is people being on their computers or phones. Therefore, in this step a team member might comment that the norm *be present* would encourage people to stay off their devices. In this way, the discussion in this step helps the group see norms as a meaningful framework for encouraging productive behaviors that support their collaborative goals.

Step 5: Revise and Add Norms

In this step, ask each participant to propose any adjustments to the baseline list of norms they feel are essential for the team's success. This includes revising, removing, or adding norms. We find that 6 to 8 norms is a reasonable number for most groups. To encourage open sharing, allow participants to write their suggestions anonymously on sticky notes, then place them on a shared board. Lead a discussion on these contributions, helping the team explore how each proposed norm might enhance or refine the group's working relationships. Facilitate a decision-making process that brings each proposed norm to a consensus or a vote as needed.

Table 8.1. Sample Working Norms for PLCs

Norm	Description	How It Supports Collaboration
Pause	Intentionally pause when speaking to allow for thoughtful response.	Allows participants to think before responding, fostering deeper understanding and reducing interruptions.
Paraphrase	Make a practice of restating what others have said in your own words.	Ensures clarity, helps others feel heard, and promotes attentive listening.
Pose Questions	Ask clarifying or probing questions to seek understanding	Encourages exploration, clarifies understanding, and deepens discussions.
Put Ideas on the Table	Offer ideas openly for group consideration.	Promotes transparency, builds trust, and encourages active participation.
Provide Evidence/Data	Use specific data and evidence to support statements.	Grounding discussions in data helps the team make informed decisions.
Pay Attention to Self and Others	Monitor your own behavior and that of the group.	Helps regulate group dynamics, ensure everyone is engaged, and promotes an outward mindset.
Presume Positive Intentions	Assume that others mean well, even during disagreements.	Builds trust, reduces defensiveness, and fosters an environment of respect.
Take Responsibility	Take responsibility for your own commitments, including any impact (intentional or not) on others.	Builds trust and ensures progress toward shared goals. Also helps people take accountability if they say or do something that bothers or offends a colleague.
Listen Actively	Focus on what others are saying without preparing a response while they speak.	Ensures understanding and demonstrates respect for others.
Be Present	Stay mentally and physically engaged in the conversation	Enhances the quality of interactions and demonstrates respect for others' time.
Respect Time Limits	Adhere to agreed-upon time limits for discussions.	Keeps meetings on schedule, showing respect for everyone's time.
Disagree Kindly and Constructively	Frame disagreements in a way that promotes problem solving rather than confrontation.	Encourages respectful exploration of different viewpoints.

(continued)

Table 8.1 (*continued*)

Norm	Description	How It Supports Collaboration
Maintain Confidentiality	Respect the confidentiality of the discussion and ensure that sensitive information stays within the group.	Builds trust among participants and fosters openness.
Stay on Topic	Focus on the issue being discussed without bringing up unrelated topics.	Keeps the conversation productive and ensures efficient use of time.

Step 6: Prioritize and Finalize Norms

Once the team has a list of potential norms, guide the team through a prioritization activity, such as Dot Voting, where each member is given 3–5 sticky dots to mark the norms they feel are most important for the group's effectiveness. The norms with the most dots win. By the end of this step, aim to have a manageable set of 6–8 prioritized norms that all members agree to uphold.

Step 7: Document and Display

Once the norms are finalized, ensure they are documented in a format that is easy to reference. Consider using chart paper, a digital platform, or a printed document to make them visible at each meeting. For example, many PLCs we work with keep norms displayed in their common meeting space. Encourage participants to refer back to these norms regularly and use them as a tool to maintain accountability and consistency in team interactions.

Step 8: Next Steps

Conclude the session by inviting each member to express their commitment to the norms. Explain that these norms will be revisited periodically to assess their effectiveness and make any necessary adjustments. Acknowledge each member's contributions and encourage everyone to hold one another accountable to uphold the norms in future meetings.

COMMON CHALLENGES AND SUGGESTIONS

Establishing or resetting PLC norms can sometimes present challenges, and it is helpful for facilitators to be prepared to address these proactively. Below we explore a few and offer suggestions.

Resistance to Norms

One common challenge is resistance to new norms, especially if participants are attached to previous norms or feel uncomfortable with change. Resistance may manifest in subtle ways, such as a lack of engagement or open skepticism. To overcome this, facilitators can emphasize the benefits of refining practices to improve collaboration and offer examples of how new norms have positively impacted other teams. It can also be helpful to invite reluctant members to share their concerns openly, ensuring that their perspectives are acknowledged and addressed. Engaging these participants by incorporating some of their suggestions into the final norms can help increase buy-in and make them feel more connected to the process.

Unbalanced Voices

Another challenge is dominance by one voice, which can stifle contributions from quieter members and lead to an imbalance in decision-making. A particularly outspoken participant might dominate discussions, leaving others hesitant to share their thoughts. Facilitators can use structured turn-taking or a round-robin format to ensure everyone has an opportunity to speak. Directly encouraging quieter participants to share their insights can help make them feel more comfortable contributing. Additionally, using tools like anonymous sticky notes or digital polls can give all members a voice without the pressure of speaking up in front of the group.

Adherence to Norms

Difficulty holding members accountable can also arise if norms are not consistently revisited or reinforced. If norms are not explicitly named or referenced, some participants may forget them or disregard their importance. Including a brief norm-check at the beginning of each meeting can remind everyone of the agreed expectations and help maintain accountability. For example, facilitators can start meetings by asking participants to reflect on how well the group upheld the norms in the previous session. Encouraging a culture of collective accountability, where members feel comfortable reminding each other of the norms, can also be effective. Facilitators should model adherence to the norms, reinforcing their significance by referencing them when issues arise and encouraging the group to do the same.

Norm Clarity

Another potential challenge is vague or unrealistic norms, which can lead to confusion or difficulty in maintaining expectations. For example, a norm like "be respectful" might be too broad for participants to understand what specific behaviors are expected. Facilitators can address this by prompting the group to clarify norms and make them more specific. Instead of "be respectful," a clearer norm could be "listen without interrupting when someone else is speaking." This level of specificity ensures that everyone knows what is expected and can hold each other accountable more effectively.

CONCLUSION

As mentioned previously, establishing effective norms is a crucial step in creating a productive and collaborative PLC. Well-defined norms lay the foundation for accountability, respect, and open communication, enabling all participants to feel heard and valued. By involving each member in shaping the norms, the team creates shared ownership, ensuring that everyone is committed to maintaining a supportive and focused working environment.

As you continue to meet with your PLC, remember that setting and resetting norms is not a one-time event but an ongoing practice or routine that evolves as the team gets comfortable working together. Norms will be most effective when they are actively referenced and reinforced, creating a culture of continuous reflection and growth. By embracing this process, PLC members will establish an environment conducive to collaboration, trust, and meaningful progress, ultimately enhancing both individual and collective professional learning.

PROTOCOL FOR ESTABLISHING PLC NORMS

Suggested Time: 60–90 Minutes

This protocol guides PLC teams in creating shared norms that promote a respectful, productive, and collaborative environment. Establishing these norms helps ensure that all meetings are effective, focused, and aligned with the team's goals.

Step 1: Establish Roles and Purpose (3 Minutes)

(1) The facilitator does the following:
- (a) States the roles needed for the session: facilitator, timekeeper, and note-taker.
- (b) Asks for volunteers or assigns roles to participants, ensuring each role is filled.
- (c) Clarifies the purpose of the meeting: to establish or reset group norms for the PLC.

Step 2: Reflect on Past Practices (10–15 Minutes)

(1) The facilitator does the following:
- (a) Asks team members to reflect on past PLC or teacher meetings and to identify and write down behaviors, decisions, or actions that have done the following:
    - Helped meetings be effective and productive.
    - Hindered meetings from being effective and productive.
- (b) Beginning with what has helped, asks team members to share their ideas.

(2) The note-taker captures notes on chart paper or a whiteboard for the group to see.

Step 3: Review Existing or Baseline Norms (5–10 Minutes)

(1) The facilitator shares a set of baseline norms and asks the team to review.
- (a) If this is the first time the team has set norms, the facilitator should share a sample set of norms (see *Table 8.1 in this chapter*).
- (b) If teams have already established a set of norms for their PLC, these should be shared and made visible to the team.

(2) After the team has reviewed the norms that have been shared, the facilitator asks for and answers any clarifying questions.

Step 4: Crosswalk Norms With Reflections (10–20 Minutes)

(1) The facilitator does the following:
  (a) Asks team members to individually identify norms from the current draft that do the following:
    - Promote helpful behaviors
    - Mitigate behaviors that hinder productivity
  (b) Once members have had time to reflect, asks members to share and discuss their ideas.

Step 5: Revise and Add Norms (15–25 Minutes)

(1) After members have discussed how the current norms help to promote desired behaviors as well as mitigate undesired behaviors, the facilitator asks members to silently consider and record the following:
  (a) Which norms from the current set to keep, remove, or revise.
  (b) New norms to add to the current set.
(2) Consider using an anonymous "sticky note" activity (physical or digital) where participants can suggest norms to keep, remove, or revise. This can encourage open and honest input.
(3) Once members have had enough time to record their ideas, the facilitator uses the following process to revise the current set of norms:
  (a) Asks for a volunteer to propose one idea—e.g., a norm to revise, keep, remove, or add.
  (b) Asks the team to discuss the idea and decide if they want to make the change (or not).
  (c) Once the team has decided, another volunteer is asked to share until all ideas have been tapped out.
(4) The note-taker keeps track of the discussion and records all norms that are agreed upon by the group.

Step 6: Prioritize and Finalize New Norms (10 Minutes)

(1) Once the new set of revised norms has been established, the facilitator asks members to review the final list.
  (a) If the list is very long, they may be asked to determine which norms could be removed.
(2) Once everyone has had time to review, the facilitator leads a discussion to ensure all participants agree with the final set of norms.

Step 7: Document and Display (3 Minutes)

(1) The note-taker documents the finalized norms in a clear and concise format.
(2) The facilitator asks the team to consider creating a visually appealing poster or digital graphic of the norms for easy reference during meetings. Displaying these norms in the regular meeting space can serve as a reminder for the team to uphold them consistently.

Step 8: Next Steps (4 Minutes)

(1) The facilitator asks each team member to share one specific way they will personally uphold the norms in future meetings, reinforcing accountability.
(2) Plan a check-in during a future meeting to review and reflect on the norms' effectiveness, adjusting as necessary to support continued productivity and respect within the PLC.

CHAPTER 9

A Protocol for Setting Student Learning Goals

INTRODUCTION

The *Protocol for Setting Student Learning Goals* is designed to guide educators through a structured process of analyzing student performance data and crafting a SMART goal for student learning. This is a key step during Phase 1 of VITAL Collaboration. As described more fully through the Theory of Improvement described in Chapter 2, establishing a goal like this is foundational to improving collective teacher efficacy. For example, a PLC of kindergarten teachers might set a student learning goal focused on improving listening comprehension. This goal could be articulated as, "By the end of the semester, 80% of students will be able to retell key details from a story they hear with 90% accuracy." Such a goal would then encourage the PLC to develop an improvement goal for themselves that focuses on enhancing their instructional practices for teaching this skill. As emphasized in earlier chapters, setting data-based learning goals is crucial for ensuring that teaching practices are aligned with student needs. This protocol supports educators in reviewing student performance data, identifying areas for growth, and crafting actionable goals that enhance both teaching and learning outcomes.

SUGGESTED TIME

The protocol typically takes 60 to 90 minutes. If time is limited, distribute student performance data beforehand so PLC members can review in advance.

MATERIALS

- The *Protocol for Setting Student Learning Goals.*
- Student-level data, such as assessment results or performance data.

- A note-taking organizer to capture observations and decisions made during the meeting.

PREPARATIONS

Before engaging in this protocol, all PLC members should be familiar with what constitutes a SMART goal. SMART goals serve as a framework for setting clear and actionable targets that directly address areas of need. For example, in a 3rd-grade PLC, a SMART goal could be, "Increase the percentage of students meeting proficiency in multiplication facts from 65% to 85% by the end of the school year through weekly timed quizzes and targeted practice sessions." If PLC members are not already familiar with SMART goals, we recommend dedicating one or two PLC sessions to learning about them. Chapter 18 in the last section of this book describes SMART goals and provides guidance on how to craft them. If teams are unfamiliar with SMART goals, we encourage them to read the chapter as a team before engaging with this protocol.

In addition to being familiar with SMART goals, facilitators should also ensure that relevant student data is shared with team members before the PLC meeting. The data selected should be both comprehensive and focused, highlighting areas of strength and areas requiring improvement. For example, sharing the results of a recent benchmark assessment in reading can help teams identify specific comprehension skills that need to be addressed.

It is also important to take a "Goldilocks" approach regarding the data provided. Too much data can be overwhelming and make it difficult to narrow down to a single target area. For instance, providing summary data on overall grade-level performance in a particular subject area can be more useful than schoolwide data across multiple content areas. Conversely, data that is too specific may make it difficult to identify and develop a broad enough goal for student progress. Keep in mind the common adage "less is more" when selecting data to analyze.

PROCESS OVERVIEW

The *Protocol for Setting Student Learning Goals* consists of seven steps that guide a PLC through a structured process for analyzing data and establishing a SMART goal. The section below walks through each step, explaining it and providing guidance.

Step 1: Determine Roles and Set Norms

The facilitator starts by clarifying roles for the meeting, such as facilitator, timekeeper, note-taker, and any other necessary roles. The facilitator then revisits the team's norms and encourages the team to select one to focus on for the day. For example, the team might emphasize the norm of *attentive listening* to encourage members to fully engage with each other's observations and insights.

Step 2: Review Data Reports and Address Clarifying Questions

The facilitator or another team member presents the PLC with student data and any relevant reports and makes sure everyone has access, either digitally or in hard copy. For instance, a teacher or data coach might present a summary of 5th-grade science assessment scores. After a brief introduction, the facilitator should allow participants to silently review the data. Encourage them to jot down any initial observations or questions they have. Following this silent review, encourage participants to ask clarifying questions about the data reports, ensuring that everyone has a clear understanding of the information in front of them.

Step 3: Examine Data

Once everyone is familiar with the data presented, PLC members silently review the data again, this time recording specific factual observations related to student performance. They might note findings such as the following:

- "40% of 7th-grade students are proficient in solving equations with one variable."
- "The average score on the last reading comprehension assessment for 4th-graders was 75%, indicating a need for targeted interventions."

It is important that all members contribute. Thus, facilitators might conduct a whip-around where each member shares one observation at a time, continuing until all relevant observations have been discussed. Encourage participants to build on each other's observations to identify patterns or trends.

Step 4: Infer and Question

After all observations have been exhausted, facilitate a discussion to draw inferences from the observations, particularly ideas about areas to target for improved growth. Facilitators should ask guiding questions such as the following:

- "What conclusions or interpretations can we draw from the data?"
- "What do the data suggest are areas to prioritize improving?"
- "What new questions arise from these interpretations?"

Keep in mind that the purpose of inferring and questioning is to begin to identify an area of student learning that would benefit from having a goal. For instance, a team might conclude that students require more practice with real-world applications of linear functions. Or a team might conclude that students need to improve in the skill of providing reasoning to back up evidence of claims in an argument.

Step 5: Set Data-Based Learning Goal

The culminating step in this protocol is to collaboratively draft a SMART student learning goal based on the inferences and interpretations drawn from the data. Ensure that the goal has the following SMART characteristics:

- **Specific**: Clearly defines the objective (e.g., "Increase the number of students proficient in solving real-world linear function problems from 55% to 75%").
- **Measurable**: Includes criteria for tracking progress (e.g., using subsequent assessments to measure proficiency).
- **Achievable**: Are realistic given available resources (e.g., instructional time and materials).
- **Relevant**: Aligns with broader educational objectives (e.g., preparing students for high school mathematics).
- **Time-bound:** Has a clear deadline for completion (e.g., "by the end of the current academic year").

As teams begin to craft a goal, facilitators should encourage their team to consider how this goal aligns with ongoing instructional improvement efforts, such as larger schoolwide goals, and to discuss strategies for achieving the goal. For instance, the team might decide to implement additional project-based learning activities that incorporate linear functions in practical scenarios. Once the goal is drafted, it should be recorded and shared with all PLC members.

Step 6: Discuss Next Steps

Outline the agenda for the next meeting. In many cases, subsequent PLC sessions will focus on developing a teaching improvement goal and/or focus on engaging in professional learning around instructional strategies aligned with the student learning goal just drafted. For example, the team might assign members to research effective instructional strategies for teaching real-world applications of linear functions and report back at the next meeting. Or members may look for research and other readings to bring back to the PLC.

Whatever is decided, the facilitator should make sure to assign responsibilities and deadlines as needed to maintain momentum.

Step 7: Debrief the Process

To conclude the discussion, participants reflect on the goal-setting process, focusing on what supported their learning and collaboration. They may also share suggestions on what could improve it in the future. Starting with the facilitator, each member shares one or more key takeaways from the session and any suggestions for refining the process in future meetings. This debrief should highlight aspects of the discussion that were most helpful, areas that might need more focus, and strategies for improving the team's approach to setting data-based student learning goals. For example, a member might note, "I found the data review step crucial in narrowing our focus, but we may need more time for the discussion around next steps next time." This reflection helps the team continuously refine the protocol, reinforcing a cycle of ongoing improvement in their collaboration.

COMMON CHALLENGES AND SOLUTIONS

Facilitators may encounter a variety of challenges when drafting goals for student learning. Many of these are associated with the different aspects of a SMART goal. Below we share some of the most common we have encountered and offer suggestions.

Specificity

One common challenge in setting SMART goals is achieving clarity around goal specificity. Teams sometimes struggle to define precisely what they want to accomplish for their students. This can result in vague goals that do not provide clear direction. For instance, a goal like "improve student performance in reading" is too general. To overcome this challenge, teams should strive to home in on concrete objectives. When this happens, facilitators can ask questions like, "What specific skills do we want our students to master?" that can help refine the student learning goal. An example of a specific goal in this area could be "increase the percentage of students scoring at or above grade level in reading fluency from 60% to 75%."

Making the Goal Measurable

Another frequent challenge PLCs encounter with goal-setting is ensuring that goals are measurable. Teams may set ambitious goals that sound impressive, but it is easy for them to lack clear criteria for measurement, making it difficult to track progress. For example, a goal stating, "students will understand fractions better" is inherently unmeasurable. To address this, teams should establish specific metrics that allow them to track progress. A revised goal might state, "Increase the number of students correctly solving fraction problems on the district's local assessments from 50% to 80% by the end of the semester."

Being Realistic

Setting realistic or achievable goals is also a challenge, as teams sometimes set their sights too high, creating expectations that are unrealistic given available resources and time. For instance, aiming for all students to achieve mastery in a complex subject area within a single month may not be feasible. Conversely, teams may set their sights too low as well. To counteract either possibility, it's crucial for teams to evaluate their current resources, including instructional time and support available. Referencing past data and performance trends can help teams can set realistic and achievable goals. For example, if a previous assessment showed that only 40–50% of students were proficient during the past 3 years, a more reasonable goal might be raising that proficiency level to 60% in the next semester or by the end of the year.

Ensuring Relevance

Ensuring the relevance of goals to broader educational objectives can also be a significant hurdle for PLCs. Creating goals that do not align with the overall needs of their students or with established curriculum standards can lead to subsequent efforts falling short of contributing effectively to teaching improvement. To ensure relevance, teams should connect their SMART goals to overarching instructional priorities. They can ask questions like, "How does this goal align with the school's overall mission and improvement plan?" For instance, a goal related to improving algebra skills should directly tie into districtwide initiatives or state standards.

Creating Manageable Timelines

Finally, teams may also struggle with establishing a clear timeline for their goals, making it difficult to maintain momentum. Goals without deadlines or with deadlines that are too far off can lead to procrastination or a lack of urgency, ultimately affecting the goal's successful implementation. To enhance accountability, teams should set specific deadlines. A revised goal could state, "Students will increase their writing scores by 10% on the next benchmark assessment by May 15," which incorporates a clear time frame. By doing so, teams create a sense of urgency and purpose in their goal-setting efforts. We often encourage PLCs to set goals for the end of a semester or the end of the school year. In short, the timeline for achieving student learning goals should allow enough time for teachers to work on enhancing their instructional practice.

CONCLUSION

In successfully following this protocol, teams will develop targeted, data-driven goals that set the stage for identifying improvements in teaching practices. The use of SMART goals ensures that the objectives for student learning are clear, focused, and actionable. Effectively setting goals in this manner provides a strong foundation for continuous improvement and helps teachers and teams identify strategic goals that support their own learning. This in turn will guide the inquiry that will take place in Phase 2 when the PLC engages in teaching and learning cycles.

PROTOCOL FOR SETTING STUDENT LEARNING GOALS

Suggested Time: 60–90 Minutes

This protocol guides PLC teams through an analysis of student data to develop a PLC-level SMART goal. This student learning goal will be used to inform a teaching improvement goal.

Step 1: Determine Roles and Set Norms (3 Minutes)

(1) Establish and clarify roles for the facilitator, timekeeper, note-taker, and any other necessary roles.
(2) Revisit the team's norms and select one to focus on for the day. Emphasize how this norm will support the effectiveness of today's session.

Step 2: Review Data Reports and Address Clarifying Questions (5–20 Minutes)

(1) Present and review student data, ensuring all participants have access to the data, either digitally or in hard copy.
(2) Allow participants to silently review the data, encouraging them to note any initial observations or questions.
(3) Facilitate a brief discussion where participants share and discuss any clarifying questions about the data reports, ensuring everyone has a clear understanding of the information presented.

Step 3: Examine Data (10–15 Minutes)

(1) Have participants silently review the data again, this time recording specific factual observations related to student performance.
(2) Conduct a round-robin where each participant shares one observation at a time, continuing until all relevant observations have been discussed. Encourage participants to build on each other's observations to identify patterns or trends.

Step 4: Infer and Question (10–20 Minutes)

(1) Facilitate a discussion to draw inferences from the observations:
    (a) What conclusions or interpretations can be drawn from the data? For example:
        (i) "The data suggest that students have mastered X concept."
        (ii) "The data indicate a need for more practice with Y skill."

  (b) What new questions arise from these interpretations?
  (c) What additional data, if any, would help to clarify or expand on these observations?

Step 5: Set Data-Based Learning Goal (10–25 Minutes)

(1) Collaboratively draft a SMART student learning goal based on the inferences and interpretations drawn from the data. Ensure that the goal is:
  (a) Specific: Clearly defines the objective.
  (b) Measurable: Includes criteria for tracking progress.
  (c) Achievable: Is realistic given available resources.
  (d) Relevant: Aligns with broader educational objectives.
  (e) Time-bound: Has a clear deadline for completion.
(2) Encourage the team to consider how this goal aligns with ongoing instructional improvement efforts and to discuss strategies for achieving the goal.

Step 6: Discuss Next Steps (3–5 Minutes)

(1) Outline the agenda for the next meeting, ensuring it includes time for monitoring progress toward the goal.
(2) Summarize the next steps, including any follow-up actions needed to support the achievement of the goal. Assign responsibilities and deadlines as needed to maintain momentum.

Step 7: Debrief the Process (4–5 Minutes)

(1) Conduct a brief reflection session where participants share their thoughts on the process:
  (a) What supported your learning during this session?
  (b) What aspects of the process could be adjusted to better support learning in future meetings?
(2) Capture key insights and suggestions for improvement and consider how they can be integrated into future sessions to enhance effectiveness.

CHAPTER 10

A Protocol for Developing Teaching Improvement Goals

INTRODUCTION

When engaging in VITAL collaboration, developing a clear goal for teacher learning is essential for driving improvements in instruction that support the student learning goal. The *Protocol for Developing Teaching Improvement Goals* introduced in this chapter is intended to be used during Phase 1 of VITAL Collaboration and guides PLCs in developing a goal for improving teaching practice that is grounded in research-based instructional practices that can directly impact student outcomes. By focusing on a targeted teaching improvement goal, PLCs establish a shared path for refining their practices and fostering a collective commitment to continuous growth.

PURPOSE

The *Protocol for Developing Teaching Improvement Goals* builds upon the foundation set by the *Protocol for Setting Student Learning Goals*. After identifying data-informed student learning goals, this protocol guides PLC teams to select specific, research-based teaching practices that directly address those student learning goals. The objective in this protocol is to align instructional strategies with student needs, ensuring a focused and effective approach to improving collective teacher efficacy on the team. By emphasizing evidence-based strategies, teams can develop a cohesive plan that promotes student achievement and continuous professional growth. Concluding Phase 1 with a clear teaching improvement goal ensures that the PLC is well-prepared to enter Phase 2, where the team will engage in teaching and learning cycles to bring these goals to fruition.

MATERIALS

- Copies of the *Protocol for Developing Teaching Improvement Goals*
- Copies of the school's and PLC's student learning goals.
- Research-based resources on effective teaching practices.
- Note-taking materials.

SUGGESTED TIME

This protocol typically requires 60 to 90 minutes. More time may be necessary if additional research on effective practices is needed.

PREPARATION

Before the session, team members should review the student learning goal or goals established during the previous protocol. Ideally, the facilitator should gather relevant research on teaching practices aligned with these goals and distribute it to all participants in advance; alternatively, the facilitator can encourage PLC members to bring research or ideas to share. This preparation ensures that everyone comes to the meeting ready to engage in a focused discussion. For example, if the PLC set a goal focused on improving students' mathematical reasoning skills, the team should review and have at the ready literature, PD resources, etc., that provide guidance around evidence-based best practice in these areas.

Educators have a variety of powerful tools at their disposal to find resources that are grounded in research and evidence-based practices. Databases such as ERIC (Education Resources Information Center, https://eric.ed.gov) provide access to peer-reviewed articles and educational research, while the practice guides produced by the Institute of Education Sciences' What Works Clearinghouse (https://ies.ed.gov/ncee/wwc/) offer actionable recommendations based on evidence. Google Scholar is another valuable tool, allowing you to search a wide range of academic research to inform your practice. Additionally, AI tools like ChatGPT can help you summarize research, generate ideas, or even explore emerging practices. Leveraging these resources will provide you with a solid foundation for identifying effective strategies aligned to the student learning goals a PLC has set.

PROCESS OVERVIEW

Below is a walk-through of each of the steps in the protocol. We encourage facilitators to read this before guiding their team through the process.

Step 1: Determine Roles and Set Norms

In this initial step, the facilitator quickly establishes roles to support a smooth and efficient session. Remind all members of the importance of adhering to the team's norms and select one norm to focus on for the day. This norm will serve as a guiding principle for the session, fostering a collaborative environment that will help maintain the team's focus on the task at hand.

Step 2: Review the Student Learning Goals

The team should begin by revisiting any established student learning goals, both at the schoolwide and PLC level. This review serves to ground the team's attention on the broader educational objectives that the teaching improvement goal should support. During this brief discussion, participants may ask clarifying questions or highlight key aspects of the student learning goals to ensure everyone is on the same page. Additionally, the team reflects on how previous teaching improvement goals have contributed to progress toward the student learning goal, identifying areas where further enhancements are needed.

Step 3: Brainstorm Teaching Practices

Step 3 forms the core of the protocol, where team members collaboratively explore various teaching practices that could effectively address the student learning goal. Each PLC member independently brainstorms a list of research-based teaching practices they believe will best support students in achieving the learning goal. These practices may include strategies such as interactive text experiences, academic discourse, formative assessments, or scaffolding techniques.

The facilitator encourages members to draw on professional learning resources provided by the school or district and to review research, such as practice guides from the *What Works Clearinghouse,* to ground their suggestions in evidence-based practice. Once individual brainstorming is complete, team members take turns sharing their ideas while the note-taker documents each contribution. During this sharing phase, the facilitator helps the group focus on practices that align most closely with the student learning goal and encourages open dialogue about the potential impact of each practice. If the team expresses uncertainty or identifies gaps in their knowledge, the facilitator may suggest engaging in additional research or professional learning before proceeding to the next step.

Step 4: Develop a Research-Based Teaching Goal

After brainstorming, the team collaborates to draft a SMART teaching improvement goal. The facilitator guides the group in ensuring that the goal is

Specific, Measurable, Achievable, Relevant, and Time-bound. The team considers how this goal aligns with ongoing student learning goals and school-level instructional improvement efforts, ensuring that their teaching goal is directly linked to the broader context of their work. This step not only creates a concrete objective for the team but also signals the end of Phase 1 of VITAL Collaboration. By setting a clear, focused goal, the team lays the groundwork for Phase 2, where they will implement and refine their teaching practices through cycles of teaching and learning.

Step 5: Discuss Next Steps

With the teaching improvement goal established, the team outlines the agenda for the next meeting, which typically involves scheduling the first teaching and learning cycle. Responsibilities should be assigned and deadlines set to maintain momentum, ensuring that the team transitions smoothly into the next phase of their collaborative work.

Step 6: Debrief the Process

In the final step, the team engages in a brief debrief to reflect on the process. The facilitator asks open-ended questions, such as, "What supported your learning during this session?" and "What aspects of the process could be adjusted to better support future meetings?" This reflection allows the team to capture insights and suggestions for improvement, fostering a culture of continuous learning. The debrief also provides closure to Phase 1 of VITAL Collaboration, reinforcing the team's readiness to engage in Phase 2's teaching and learning cycles.

COMMON CHALLENGES AND SOLUTIONS

As with the *Protocol for Setting Student Learning Goals,* facilitators may encounter challenges when facilitating this protocol. Below we describe a few of these and suggest strategies for addressing them.

Vague or Unrealistic Goals

Setting adult learning goals focused on enhancing professional practice can present unique challenges, particularly when translating broad instructional goals into focused, actionable steps. One common challenge is creating goals that are too vague or unrealistic. Teams often grapple with defining objectives that are clear and measurable while remaining attainable. To address this, the facilitator should guide the team through the SMART criteria during goal-setting. Encouraging the use of specific language and measurable indicators helps maintain clarity and feasibility. For instance, instead of setting a broad goal like "improve questioning techniques," the team might refine it to "incorporate open-ended questions into all lessons during the next three months." This specificity provides a concrete target that the team can work toward and monitor.

Ensuring Alignment

Another challenge lies in ensuring alignment between the teaching improvement goal and established student learning goals. Sometimes, the discussion may veer off into practices that, while valuable, do not directly address the identified student needs. To mitigate this, the facilitator should revisit the student learning goals at the beginning of the session and continually frame the brainstorming around these goals. It may also be helpful to share and review the Theory of Improvement described in Chapter 2, which illustrates the close relationship between student learning goals and teaching improvement goals. By anchoring the conversation to student needs, the team can maintain a clear focus on setting adult learning goals that will have the most significant impact on student outcomes.

Identifying Effective Strategies

Limited access to research-based strategies can also hinder the goal-setting process. Teams may find it difficult to identify effective teaching practices due to a lack of resources or familiarity with current research. In these cases, the facilitator's role is crucial in preparing for the session by gathering research-based resources and sharing them with the team in advance. Professional development focused on evidence-based strategies can expand the team's knowledge base, providing them with a toolkit of practices to draw upon when setting their teaching improvement goals. If professional development is needed, we encourage facilitators to take time to do this between the setting of student goals and developing a teaching improvement goal.

Follow-Through

Lastly, follow-through is often a concern, especially when teams set ambitious adult learning goals without a clear plan for implementation. During the "Next Steps" discussion, the facilitator should emphasize the importance of scheduling the teaching and learning cycles that will take place during Phase 2. In addition, incorporating regular check-ins during future meetings to monitor progress will help keep the PLC accountable and allow for timely adjustments if necessary.

CONCLUSION

The *Protocol for Developing Teaching Improvement Goals* marks the culmination of Phase 1 in VITAL Collaboration. By setting specific, research-based goals for adult learning, PLCs create a focused path for enhancing instructional practice. This protocol not only aligns the team's efforts with student learning goals but also prepares them for the next phase of their work. As teams move into Phase 2 and begin to engage in teaching and learning cycles, they do so with a clear objective that guides their practice and promotes intentionality in their instructional strategies.

PROTOCOL FOR DEVELOPING TEACHING IMPROVEMENT GOALS

Suggested Time: 60–90 Minutes

This protocol guides PLC teams through a process to develop a PLC-level goal for improving teaching practice that is aligned with the team's student learning goal. The teaching improvement goal will be used to organize the teaching and learning cycles in Phase 2.

Step 1: Determine Roles and Set Norms (2 Minutes)

(1) Establish and clarify roles for the facilitator, timekeeper, note-taker, and any other necessary roles.
(2) Revisit the team's norms and select one to focus on for the day. Emphasize how this norm will support the effectiveness of today's session.

Step 2: Review Student Learning Goals (3 Minutes)

(1) Review any student learning goals previously established by the school or the PLC.
(2) Address any clarifying questions about the goals.

Step 3: Brainstorm Teaching Practices (30–45 Minutes)

(1) Each PLC member individually brainstorms and makes a list of teaching practices that would most likely help students meet the learning goal. Teaching practices refer to pedagogical approaches that have been shown to support learning (e.g., interactive text experience, academic discourse, formative assessment, scaffolding, etc.).
    (a) If helpful, teams may wish to draw on professional learning provided by your school or district. Other options are to review research and resources such as practice guides from the What Works Clearinghouse.
(2) Once everyone is ready, have PLC members take turns sharing their ideas as the note-taker takes notes.
(3) Once everyone has shared, the facilitator asks team members if they are ready to set a teaching goal or if the team needs to do additional research and meet again.
    (a) If ready, move to the next step.
    (b) If not, plan to continue doing research or to engage in additional professional learning.

Step 4: Set a Research-Based Teaching Goal (20–30 Minutes)

(1) Collaboratively draft a SMART teaching improvement goal based on the ideas generated. Ensure that the goal is:
  (a) *Specific*: Clearly defines the objective.
  (b) *Measurable*: Includes criteria for tracking progress.
  (c) *Achievable*: Is realistic given available resources.
  (d) *Relevant*: Aligns with broader educational objectives.
  (e) *Time-bound*: Has a clear deadline for completion.

(2) Encourage the team to consider how this goal aligns with ongoing existing student learning goals, as well as any school level instructional improvement efforts.

Step 5: Discuss Next Steps (2–5 Minutes)

(1) Outline the agenda for the next meeting, ensuring it includes time for monitoring progress toward the goal and setting up a TLC cycle.

(2) Summarize the next steps, including any follow-up actions needed to support the achievement of the goal. Assign responsibilities and deadlines as needed to maintain momentum.

Step 6: Debrief the Process (3–5 Minutes)

(1) Conduct a brief reflection session where participants share their thoughts on the process:
  (a) What supported your learning during this session?
  (b) What aspects of the process could be adjusted to better support learning in future meetings?

(2) Capture key insights and suggestions for improvement and consider how they can be integrated into future sessions to enhance effectiveness.

CHAPTER 11

A Protocol for Analyzing Standards

INTRODUCTION

The *Protocol for Analyzing Standards* is a structured process that brings educators together to collaboratively dissect and interpret academic standards. It is an important part of a teaching and learning cycle in Phase 2 of VITAL Collaboration. This protocol not only helps to ensure that teachers have a common and consistent understanding of the standards their lessons are designed to teach; it also promotes in-depth discussion about what the standards imply for teaching. By aligning expectations set forth in the standards with the desired outcomes of lessons, teachers can better design lessons that effectively address the skills and knowledge students need to succeed.

PURPOSE

The purpose of the *Protocol for Analyzing Standards* is to generate a common understanding of the knowledge and skills students are expected to master in the standards that are the focus of lessons. Standards are notoriously difficult to understand, as they are often ambiguous and overly complicated. If a PLC is using this protocol for the first time, we encourage them to read the Chapter 19, "Why Standards Are Difficult to Understand," in Part IV of this book.

SUGGESTED TIME

In most contexts, it takes 60–90 minutes to analyze a standard. In short, the longer and more complex the standard, the longer it takes to analyze it. Sometimes it is necessary to spend two PLC meetings to unpack a complex standard.

MATERIALS

- The *Protocol for Analyzing Standards*
- Copies of the standard or standards to be focused on, as well as any adjacent standards from earlier and subsequent grade levels. In many schools it is important to have both the content standards and English Language Development standards.
- Chart paper or a digital tool for collaborative note-taking.
- Highlighters and sticky notes or annotation tools to mark key elements of the standards.
- Copies of a note-taker or record sheet for documenting insights and instructional implications.

PREPARATION

In advance of the PLC session, the facilitator should identify the focus standard that the team will analyze, ensuring that it is a standard relevant to a current instructional focus. Often it is the main standard from a lesson that will be tuned in an upcoming PLC as part of a teaching and learning cycle. It is not always necessary to analyze a standard in its entirety, just as it is not always necessary or even viable to teach all aspects of a standard during a lesson. Thus, it may be helpful to identify which part of a standard will be focused on for analysis. For example, see Figure 11.1 below. It illustrates how we recommend writing a standard to show which parts are to be analyzed. As the figure shows, the second half of the standard has been struck out indicating that this section is not the focus for analysis.

It may also be helpful to gather related standards from adjacent grade levels to provide context for vertical alignment. If possible, teachers should review these standards prior to the meeting and think about how they already address these expectations in their classrooms.

Figure 11.1. How to Indicate the Parts of a Standard to Analyze

Reading Informational Text (Grades 9–10)- CCSS.ELA-LITERACY.RI.9-10.8: Delineate and evaluate the argument and specific claims in a text, assessing whether the reasoning is valid, and the evidence is relevant and sufficient; ~~identify false statements and fallacious reasoning.~~

PROCESS OVERVIEW

The following section provides an overview and guidance for each step in the *Protocol for Analyzing Standards*. Each step is critical to ensure that standards are fully understood, and instructional and assessment strategies are well aligned to them.

Step 1: Determine Roles and Set Norms

Begin by assigning roles such as facilitator, timekeeper, and recorder. Revisit group norms to foster an environment conducive to collaboration and open discussion. For example, encourage all members to contribute equally and remind the group that all questions are welcome. Reaffirming the norms helps ensure that everyone understands their responsibilities and contributes productively.

Step 2: Clarify the Standard(s) for Analysis

Guide the team in clarifying the standards that will be analyzed. It is often preferable to focus on one primary content standard, but where teachers are required to have English Language Development (ELD) standards aligned to the standards in each lesson, include those as well. For instance, if the content standard focuses on "analyzing informational texts," an aligned ELD standard could involve "using language to explain and analyze ideas in text."

Step 3: Unpack the Content Standard

Break down the selected content standard into its key components by discussing the concepts and knowledge as well as processes and skills students are expected to learn. A note-taking tool is provided with the protocol to assist with this.

When analyzing the knowledge elements, distinguish between declarative, procedural, and conditional knowledge. *Declarative* knowledge includes the facts and information students need to memorize. *Procedural* knowledge involves understanding the steps of a process. *Conditional* knowledge refers to knowing when and how to apply both declarative and procedural knowledge to complete a task effectively. See Table 11.1 for a sample breakdown of these knowledge types for the first part of a Grade 4 math standard.

When analyzing the skills in a standard, it is helpful to initially focus on the verbs, as well as what is stated and implied in the standard. For example, in the standard showcased in Table 11.1, the key verb "solve" is indicating that

Table 11.1. Sample Breakdown of Different Kinds of Knowledge in a Math Standard

Operations and Algebraic Thinking (Grade 4)- 4.OA.A.3 *Solve multistep word problems posed with whole numbers using the four operations, including problems in which remainders must be interpreted.*
Declarative Knowledge Students need to **memorize facts** such as the four operations (addition, subtraction, multiplication, division) and basic terms like "remainder" and "whole number."
Procedural Knowledge Students need to **understand the steps** required to solve multistep word problems. This includes identifying the operations needed, performing calculations, and interpreting the remainder if present.
Conditional Knowledge Students need to **understand when and how to apply** different operations to solve a given problem. For example, students must decide whether to add or multiply first based on the context of the word problem and know how to interpret the remainder correctly based on the problem's requirements.

the students need to be able to demonstrate the ability to independently figure out the answer to multistep word problems. Often implied in this standard is the ability to demonstrate this multiple times. In addition, many teachers agree they want students to also be able to *explain* their reasoning.

Step 4: (Optional) Unpack the English Language Development Standard

If applicable, select an ELD standard that aligns with the content standard to analyze as well. Discuss how this standard will support English learners in accessing the content effectively. For example, if the content standard is about "writing an argumentative essay," the ELD standard could focus on "using language to express opinions and provide evidence." Discuss how scaffolding strategies, such as sentence frames, can be used to help English learners meet the language demands of the content standard. Follow the same procedures in Step 3 for analyzing the ELD standard.

Step 5: Discuss Instructional Implications

Next, consider the instructional strategies that best align with the unpacked standards. Discuss ways to teach the content effectively and engage all students. For example, if the content standard involves "comparing themes in literature," teachers might use graphic organizers to help students visualize similarities and differences. This step helps ensure that teachers are prepared to implement instructional practices that support all learners in mastering the standards.

Step 6: Discuss Assessment Implications

In addition to discussing the instructional implications of the standards, also consider how mastery of the standard will be assessed. Discuss different types of assessments (formative and summative) and ensure they align with the rigor and intent of the standard. For example, if students are expected to "justify their mathematical reasoning," a formative assessment could involve having students explain their thinking in writing or verbally during a class discussion. Use examples of assessment tasks to clarify expectations for measuring student progress.

Step 7: Determine Next Steps

Identify actionable next steps for integrating the standard into instruction. The most typical next step in a teaching and learning cycle is for a teacher to bring a lesson that is designed to teach the standard just analyzed.

Step 8: Debrief the Process

Reflect on the effectiveness of the protocol. Discuss what went well, such as clear alignment of strategies, and what could be improved for future sessions. Consider how the insights gained will inform instructional planning. For example, the facilitator might ask, "What was one takeaway that will impact your planning next week?" This reflection helps the team refine its collaborative practices and improve future standards analysis.

COMMON CHALLENGES AND SOLUTIONS

While the *Protocol for Analyzing Standards* is designed to be a straightforward process, challenges may arise. Below is a brief description of the more common of these with suggestions on how to address them if they arise.

Overwhelming Complexity of Standards

Some standards may seem overly complex or broad, which can make analysis daunting. In these cases, it's helpful to break the standard into smaller, more manageable components as illustrated through the strikethrough in Figure 11.1 above. By isolating part of the standard, teachers can focus on one element of the standard at a time, ensuring that each part is fully understood before moving on to the next.

Misalignment in Interpretation

Different teachers may have varying interpretations of the same standard, which can lead to confusion or miscommunication. To mitigate this, facilitators should encourage open dialogue where everyone's perspective is valued. Using the standards from the grade levels before and after for comparison can also help clarify ambiguities. When there are conflicting interpretations, it is essential to come to agreement and to record the consensus for future reference.

Time Constraints

Given the depth of discussion required, time is often a concern. One solution is to prioritize key parts of the standard that need immediate attention and save less critical components for future discussions. Alternatively, the PLC facilitator can schedule follow-up sessions if the standard needs more thorough analysis.

CONCLUSION

In this chapter, we introduced the *Protocol for Analyzing Standards*, emphasizing its importance in ensuring that teachers have a shared understanding of the knowledge and skills students need to develop. By breaking down standards, discussing instructional and assessment implications, and planning next steps, teacher teams can align their teaching practices more closely with student needs. This protocol also sets the PLC up for success when tuning a lesson where the standard just analyzed is the focus. This is the focus of Chapter 12.

PROTOCOL FOR ANALYZING STANDARDS

Suggested Time: 60–90 Minutes
This protocol guides PLC teams through a process for analyzing a standard. This analysis prepares PLCs to tune a lesson during the next part of a TLC.

Step 1: Determine Roles and Set Norms (2 Minutes)

(1) Establish and clarify roles for the facilitator, timekeeper, note-taker, and any other necessary roles.
(2) Revisit the team's norms and select one to focus on for the day. Emphasize how this norm will support the effectiveness of today's session.

Step 2: Identify the Standard(s) for Analysis (3 Minutes)

(1) Identify and record the complete text of each standard to be focused on for analysis. If analyzing only part of a standard, underline this and/or strike out parts not to be analyzed.

Step 3: Unpack the Content Standard (20–30 Minutes)

(1) Analyze, or "unpack," the academic expectations in the content standards. Record responses on the Analyzing Standards Note-taking Tool (below). Do the following:
  (a) **Unpack concepts and knowledge**—Begin by looking for key nouns.
    (i) Identify concepts and knowledge that students should already have from mastering previous standards.
    (ii) Identify stated or implied concepts and knowledge that students need to learn and be taught.
  (b) **Unpack processes and skills**—Begin by looking for key verbs.
    (i) Identify stated or implied processes and skills that students need to learn and be taught.
    (ii) Identify the processes and skills that students should already have from mastering previous standards.

Step 4: (Optional) Unpack the English Language Development Standard (20–25 Minutes)

(1) Follow the same procedures from Step 3 to analyze the English Language Development standard. Record responses on the Analyzing Standards Note-taking Tool.

Step 5: Discuss Instructional Implications (5–10 Minutes)

(1) Consider the implications for instruction on both content and language.
(2) Brainstorm ideas and strategies for teaching the concepts, knowledge, skills, processes, and language.

Step 6: Discuss Assessment Implications (5–10 Minutes)

(1) Consider and discuss the implications for assessment.
   (a) Brainstorm ideas and strategies for assessing the concepts, knowledge, skills, and processes.
   (b) Consider how to assess both content and language learning and what strategies can be used to measure them.
   (c) If analyzing an ELD standard as well, refer to proficiency level descriptors that are usually part of the standards framework to better understanding of what assessment might look like for different language proficiency levels.

Step 7: Determine Next Steps (2–5 Minutes)

(1) Summarize next steps based on the results of the meeting. If the PLC is engaging in a TLC, a logical next step is to engage in lesson tuning.
(2) Outline the agenda for next meeting.

Step 8: Debrief the Process (3–5 Minutes)

(1) Share and discuss reflections and insights about the process and from the conversation.
   (a) What supported your learning?
   (b) What could we adjust next time we meet to better support your learning?

ANALYZING STANDARDS NOTE-TAKING TOOL

Content Standard

CONCEPTS & KNOWLEDGE (NOUNS)	**PROCESSES & SKILLS (VERBS)**
Declarative, Procedural, Conditional - *What knowledge should students already have?* -	- *What skills should students already have?* -

Aligned ELD Standard

CONCEPTS & KNOWLEDGE (NOUNS)	**PROCESSES & SKILLS (VERBS)**
Declarative, Procedural, Conditional - *What knowledge should students already have?* -	- *What skills should students already have?* -

IMPLICATIONS FOR INSTRUCTION (Ideas for Teaching)

-

IMPLICATIONS FOR ASSESSMENT (Ideas for Assessing)

CHAPTER 12

A Protocol for Tuning a Lesson

INTRODUCTION

The *Protocol for Tuning a Lesson* is an essential component of the Teaching and Learning Cycle that is central to Phase 2 within the VITAL Collaboration framework. This protocol guides teachers through a structured process to present, analyze, and refine lessons in collaboration with peers to cultivate feedback that will drive improvements in practice. Lessons that are the focus of tuning can be either teacher-generated or a lesson from a published curriculum resource. Ideally, lessons presented for tuning will be attempting to integrate new strategies or techniques that are aligned to a PLC's teaching improvement goal. For example, a PLC that has a goal of improving how teachers teach listening comprehension would be well positioned to tune lessons that focus on or include new techniques for teaching this skill, like using anchor charts with key words that help students construct images as they listen to a teacher read.

PURPOSE

The purpose of the *Protocol for Tuning a Lesson* is to create space for a teacher to share a lesson and get feedback before teaching it. This creates an opportunity to improve the lesson before it is taught. Within the VITAL Collaboration framework, this protocol is a tool for educators to examine instructional design, ensuring lessons are both standards-driven and tailored to student needs. By using this protocol, teachers gain insights from their colleagues, who are well-positioned to help them refine their approach and implement changes that enhance student outcomes. This process reinforces the VITAL framework's commitment to structured, rigorous, and ongoing professional growth that strengthens collective efficacy.

SUGGESTED TIME

The protocol typically takes 60–90 minutes to complete. The length of time depends on the group size and the lesson's complexity.

MATERIALS

- The *Protocol for Tuning a Lesson*
- Copies of the lesson to be tuned
- Copies of note-taking sheets to record feedback
- Completed Prep Sheet from the presenting teacher
- Notes from any previous analysis of the focus standard(s) in the lesson

PREPARATION

The presenting teacher plays a pivotal role in setting the stage for a successful tuning session. Before the meeting, they should select a lesson they want to refine and complete a Prep Sheet that provides an overview of the lesson. Ideally, we encourage presenting teachers to spend 15–30 minutes preparing. A prep sheet template is provided below. This sheet helps the teacher to reflect on key aspects of their lesson, such as the student background, the objectives, alignment with standards, and specific elements they seek feedback on. Completing the prep sheet in advance encourages the presenting teacher to approach the session with clarity and purpose, ensuring that the discussion is targeted and productive.

In addition to the prep sheet, the presenting teacher should share in advance or have copies of the lesson to pass out to PLC members during the meeting. Often we are asked how big or small the lesson should be. We recommend the lesson focus on an instructional section for a single class or episode of instruction, as compared to a unit. Usually, a lesson that is intended to last 45–60 minutes hits the sweet spot.

For their part, the facilitator should review the protocol steps and the presenting teacher's completed prep sheet before the session, as well as any notes from previous analysis of the standards focused on in the lesson. In addition, if the facilitator is new to facilitating this protocol, we encourage them to read the process overview below prior to facilitating. This preparation allows the facilitator to guide the group effectively through each phase of the protocol, keeping the focus on constructive dialogue that aligns with the VITAL framework's standards-based approach.

PROCESS OVERVIEW

The guidance below provides insights and suggestions for executing each step of the *Protocol for Tuning a Lesson*.

Step 1: Determine Roles and Revisit Norms

The facilitator kicks off the protocol by assigning or clarifying the key roles to ensure a structured session. Key roles include the presenter, timekeeper, note-taker, and process observer. The facilitator should revisit the group norms, reminding participants of the importance of creating a supportive, respectful environment. Reaffirming norms such as attentive listening and positive intentions helps to establish a tone of trust and collaboration, all essential components of the VITAL framework.

Step 2: Present Materials

The presenting teacher provides an overview of the lesson using their completed prep sheet. The facilitator should encourage the presenter to be brief and remind PLC members to hold clarifying questions until later. The presenter should focus on sharing information that will help the team understand the lesson being put on the table. This may include important background information about the class and students' needs, the lesson's objectives, and how student learning will be measured, as well as a brief overview of the instructional sequence. This initial presentation helps situate the group in the context of the lesson and sets the focus for the feedback session, aligning the discussion with standards and instructional goals.

Step 3: Review Lesson Materials

After the presenter has introduced the lesson, all participants silently review it and any materials provided by the presenting teacher. This step provides process time and allows each member to familiarize themselves with the lesson's content, standards, objectives, materials, and pacing. Taking a moment for silent review ensures that everyone is on the same page and prepares them for a more informed discussion.

Step 4: Clarify Materials

When everyone has had time to understand the lesson that was presented, PLC members may ask clarifying questions to gain a better understanding of the lesson. Keep in mind that clarifying questions are intended to be straightforward, prompting short, concise responses from the presenter. This step ensures that the group has a clear understanding of the lesson before moving into deeper analysis, echoing the VITAL framework's emphasis on data-informed inquiry. It is quite common for clarifying questions to evolve into more probing questions; this may be a sign that the team understands what has been shared and is ready to move to Step 5.

Step 5: Review the Focus Standards

The presenting teacher introduces the focus standard(s) aligned with the lesson. If the standard was previously unpacked (which is preferred), the group can quickly revisit the notes from that analysis to remind themselves of the knowledge and skills required and the implications for teaching and assessing. If the standard has not been previously analyzed, the group must now work together to identify and discuss the knowledge and skills students need to meet the standard. In sum, this step works to anchor the discussion in standards, supporting the VITAL framework's focus on aligning instruction with clear learning objectives. If the standard has not already been analyzed, a second PLC session will probably be needed to complete the full lesson tuning process.

Step 6: Determine the Focus for Feedback

Once everyone has a clear understanding of the lesson and its objectives, the presenter should identify a specific element of the lesson or pose a question for the group to consider during the feedback phase. This step ensures that the feedback remains targeted and relevant, aligning with the VITAL framework's goal of purposeful reflection. The facilitator should encourage the presenting teacher to request feedback that aligns with the PLC's teaching improvement goal.

Step 7: Tune the Lesson

Once the focus for feedback is clear, participants silently review the lesson materials again, using a structured approach to recording feedback. It is important to make sure team members have sufficient time to analyze the lesson and record their feedback.

Once everyone is ready, the group begins to give feedback by first sharing praise for effective practices in the lesson, followed by probing questions and suggestions for improvement. (Regardless of the approach taken for organizing feedback, always include and begin with praise and the naming of what is working and effective about the lesson.) The presenting teacher listens to the feedback, focusing on gathering insights for refining their instruction. The facilitator should work to ensure the conversation remains positive, constructive, and aligned with the standards and learning objectives discussed earlier. This phase embodies VITAL's commitment to collaborative, reflective dialogue focused on enhancing instructional practice.

Step 8: Lesson Reflection

After the sharing and discussion of feedback, the presenting teacher shares their takeaways, learnings, and actions they will take as a result of the discussion. Following this, other PLC members reflect on their own learning from the session. This reflection reinforces the VITAL framework's focus on continuous improvement, providing an opportunity for all participants to internalize the insights gained during the tuning process.

Step 9: Plan for Observation (If Applicable)

If the team plans to observe the lesson, the next step is to discuss what evidence of student learning they will look for, what teaching behaviors will be recorded, and when and where the observation will take place. This step allows the group to extend the tuning session into the classroom, emphasizing VITAL's principle of using data to inform instructional practice.

Step 10: Plan for Analyzing Student Work (If Applicable)

If the team intends to analyze student work from the lesson, they should also determine what work the presenting teacher will collect. It is often not necessary to gather work from every student; a representative sample will suffice. It all depends on the nature and complexity of the student work generated. Plan to gather an appropriate amount of work that can be analyzed in a future PLC.

Step 11: Determine Next Steps

As the PLC comes to a close, the facilitator works with the team to outline the agenda for the next meeting. Based on the discussion from the previous two steps, they should consider the protocol to be used, clarify preparation tasks, and assign responsibilities. By clarifying next steps, the team maintains momentum and ensures that the insights from the tuning session are carried forward into future collaboration.

Step 12: Debrief

To finish the meeting, participants, beginning with the presenting teacher, share reflections about the process itself. The team should discuss what aspects supported their learning and suggest adjustments for future sessions. This final debriefing reinforces VITAL's emphasis on reflective practice and promotes continuous refinement of collaborative processes.

COMMON CHALLENGES AND SOLUTIONS

As with any collaborative process, challenges can and often do arise during the lesson tuning process that may hinder its effectiveness. Awareness of these potential issues can help facilitators anticipate and navigate them, ensuring a constructive and focused session. Below are common challenges with suggestions for addressing them.

Unclear Focus for Feedback

One common challenge is an unclear or overly broad focus for feedback. When the presenter does not clearly identify a specific element of the lesson or question for the group to consider, the discussion can become unfocused, reducing its impact. An unclear focus for feedback makes it difficult for team members to provide it. Another important reason for having the presenting teacher identify a focus for feedback is that this creates a permission structure for colleagues to provide it. It also increases the likelihood the presenting teacher will embrace the feedback given. When the focus for feedback is unclear, it weakens the permission structure and decreases the likelihood that feedback will be meaningful and aligned to what the presenting teacher wants and needs. Presenters can use the prep sheet to reflect on their lesson beforehand and pinpoint areas where they seek targeted feedback. The facilitator can further support this process by prompting the presenter to clarify their focus before moving into the tuning session. Prompts that help include the questions, "Can you tell us a little more about what would be most helpful to you?" and "Can you give an example of the type of feedback you are hoping to receive?" Or, "What kind of feedback would help us make progress toward our teaching improvement goal?"

Too Much Presenter Talk

Another issue arises when the presenting teacher talks too much during the session. The more they talk, the less space there is for discussion and feedback. For example, they might provide an overly detailed introduction or respond to every comment during feedback, which can disrupt the flow of the discussion. This behavior often stems from feelings of nervousness or discomfort with sharing their work. While the presenter's voice is important, the facilitator should gently remind them that their role during the feedback phase is primarily to listen. Emphasizing that the session is a collective effort to support growth can help the presenter feel more at ease, encouraging them to focus on gathering insights from their peers. Lastly, if a facilitator senses nervousness on the part of the presenting teacher, they should ensure that practices such as depersonalizing language, described in Chapter 5, are used. One tactic we have found helpful is to acknowledge that sharing one's professional work, like a lesson, can be scary and that doing so is an act of courage and a model of professionalism.

Giving Constructive Feedback Early

During the clarifying questions phase, participants sometimes start giving constructive feedback prematurely. This often signals that the group has understood the lesson and is eager to move forward. While this enthusiasm is positive, the facilitator should guide the team back to asking clarifying questions to ensure a thorough understanding of the lesson's context before diving into feedback. Only when there are no more clarifying questions should the facilitator move the team to the next step.

A related challenge occurs when participants become too critical or offer constructive feedback too quickly. While actionable feedback is vital, the tone and timing are equally important. Facilitators can address this by emphasizing the importance of beginning with praise and encouraging the use of sentence starters that promote a balanced discussion. Reminding the group that the protocol aims to support the presenter's growth helps maintain a constructive and positive atmosphere.

Each of these challenges can be managed through skilled facilitation and clear communication of norms. By being mindful of these potential pitfalls, facilitators and participants can ensure that the lesson tuning process remains a valuable and productive experience, fully aligned with the VITAL framework's focus on high-quality collaboration.

CONCLUSION

The *Protocol for Tuning a Lesson* is a powerful tool within Phase 2 of the VITAL Collaboration framework, directly supporting the teaching and learning cycle. By providing a structured, standards-driven approach to lesson analysis and feedback, it empowers teachers to continuously refine their practice, particularly when aligned to the PLC's teaching improvement goal. When embedded into regular PLC meetings, the protocol fosters a culture of reflective dialogue and shared professional growth, ultimately enhancing both instructional practice and student learning outcomes. Through consistent use of this protocol, educators can actively engage in the cycle of reflection and improvement that is at the heart of VITAL Collaboration.

PREP SHEET FOR LESSON TUNING

Presenting Teacher:
Content / Grade:

Directions

This sheet is designed to help PLC members who will be presenting a lesson for feedback from their peers during the lesson tuning process. To help optimize the time, do the following.

1. Analyze the focus standard(s) of the lesson in advance by using the *Analyzing Standards Note-taking Tool* in Chapter 11.
2. Respond to the pre-tuning prompts below. They are designed to help presenting teachers prepare for describing the lesson succinctly during the lesson tuning process.
3. Share everything in advance with your PLC colleagues in advance of the PLC meeting, or have everything ready to share at the beginning of the meeting.

Presentation Prompts

1. Briefly describe the lesson. Focus on explaining the instructional sequence of activities.
2. Describe the students who will be engaging in the lesson, including notable learning needs. Consider sharing recent student work or formative assessment data.
3. List potential areas of confusion students may have.
4. To what extent does the lesson target all or part of the focus standard(s)?
5. To what extent does the lesson support or address other standards?
6. What feedback would be most helpful to receive from your colleagues about the lesson?

PROTOCOL FOR TUNING A LESSON

Suggested Time: 60–90 Minutes

This protocol guides PLC teams through a process for tuning a lesson. This protocol is designed to provide feedback before a lesson is taught and prepares the team to observe the lesson in action.

Step 1: Determine Roles and Revisit Norms (2 Minutes)

(1) The facilitator identifies and makes sure everyone is clear about their role—for example, presenter, timekeeper, note-taker, and process observer.
(2) The facilitator revisits norms as needed.

Step 2: Present Materials (3-10 Minutes)

(1) The presenter does the following:
 (a) Provides important background information about specific classes and students' needs, including any recent student work and/or formative assessment data.
 (b) Describes the objective of the lesson
 (c) Explains how student learning will be measured.
 (d) Provides a brief overview and description of the lesson.

Step 3: Review Lesson Materials (2 Minutes)

(1) All members silently review lesson materials.

Step 4: Clarify Materials (3 Minutes)

(1) PLC members ask clarifying questions that prompt answers with quick, preferably yes/no responses.

Step 5: Review the Focus Standards (10 Minutes)

(1) The presenting teacher introduces the focus standard that aligns to this lesson.
 (a) If the standard was already unpacked, review the Analyzing Standards Note-taking Tool to discuss the knowledge and skills that apply to this lesson.
 (b) If the standard was not analyzed previously, identify and discuss the knowledge and skills needed for this lesson.

Step 6: Determine the Focus for Feedback (1–3 Minutes)

(1) The presenter poses a question or identifies an element of the lesson for the group to focus on to guide feedback.

Step 7: Tune the Lesson (20–25 Minutes)

(1) PLC members silently review the lesson again and record feedback.
(2) Share praise of effective practice.
(3) Share and discuss probing questions, constructive feedback, and actions for strengthening collective practice.

Step 8: Lesson Reflection (5 Minutes)

(1) The presenting teacher shares their takeaways, learnings, and actions they will take as a result of the discussion.
(2) The other PLC members share their takeaways and learnings.

Step 9: Plan for Observation (If Applicable) (5–10 Minutes)

(1) If the team plans to observe the lesson, the following should be discussed in advance.
  (a) What evidence of student learning will be looked for?
  (b) What teaching behaviors will be recorded and how?
  (c) When and where will the observation take place?

Step 10: Plan for Analyzing Student Work (If Applicable) (5–10 Minutes)

(1) If the team plans to analyze student work from the lesson, then it should be determined what work will be collected by the presenting teacher.

Step 11: Next Steps (2–5 Minutes)

(1) The facilitator works with the team to outline the agenda for next meeting. Consider:
  (a) What protocol will we use?
  (b) What preparation tasks need to happen in advance?
  (c) Who will be responsible for what?
(2) Participants clarify and share their next steps as a result of this meeting.

Step 12: Debrief (2–5 Minutes)

(1) Beginning with the presenting teacher, participants share reflections about the process. Consider the following:
  (a) What supported your learning?
  (b) What could be adjusted next time to better support our learning?

CHAPTER 13

A Protocol for Discussing a Classroom Observation

INTRODUCTION

The *Protocol for Discussing a Classroom Observation* is designed to provide a structured process for analyzing instruction observed during a peer observation. Many PLCs use the protocol after a lesson has been tuned and observed by members of the PLC. Once the lesson has been taught and observed, PLC members use this protocol to share observations, offer praise, and provide formative (non-evaluative) feedback to support the team's progress toward their teaching improvement goal. Much like the tuning protocol, this protocol walks PLC members through a process of sharing observations, analyzing data from what transpired in a lesson, and then providing feedback to the teacher of record.

PURPOSE

The purpose of the *Protocol for Discussing a Classroom Observation* is to create a structured opportunity for a teacher to receive constructive feedback from peers. Ideally, the feedback is aligned to a PLC's teaching and learning goal. Whereas the *Protocol for Tuning a Lesson* aims to provide feedback on the design of a lesson, the observation protocol provides feedback around the actual implementation of it. This protocol is a core component of a teaching and learning cycle as it provides feedback on the most important aspect of teaching practice: instruction. This protocol also sets PLCs up for the final conversation in a complete teaching and learning cycle: analyzing student work.

SUGGESTED TIME

This protocol takes 60–90 minutes, depending on the size of the group and the depth of discussion. The process can be adjusted to fit shorter time frames if needed.

MATERIALS

- The *Protocol for Discussing a Classroom Observation*
- Observation Notes

PREPARATIONS

Preparations for this protocol typically begin toward the end of the lesson tuning process, when teams make a plan for observing the lesson just tuned. In some schools, scheduling when a lesson will be observed is simple. In other locations, it takes substantial coordination to arrange coverage for PLC members to allow them to observe one of their colleagues.

In some cases, it is not feasible for teachers to observe the lesson live. When this happens, we recommend videorecording the lesson. The simplest way to use video is for the teacher being observed to record the lesson or a portion of it and share it with their team; there are also commercial platforms and websites that allow individuals to record a video and share it with colleagues in a secure space. Many of these platforms also allow for collaborative marking and annotation of videos, similar to using the comment feature in a Word or Google document. For example, teachers can share videos via YouTube using the "unlisted" option to maintain privacy. This option makes videos available only to those who have the link and allows viewers to comment. Another platform we like to use is VideoANT (https://ant.umn.edu), developed by the University of Minnesota, which allows teachers to share videos with closed groups, who can then watch the video and tag specific moments with comments.

Once your teams has determined when a lesson will be observed, make a plan for what data will be collected. First, the teacher being observed should indicate what kind of feedback they are seeking. Ideally, this will align with the PLC's teaching improvement goal. Once the team understands the kind of feedback the teacher is looking for, PLC members can decide what type of data to collect. For example, one member might focus on recording everything the teacher says and does, while another might focus on what students say and do. In a lesson involving multiple groups, teachers may divide the groups among themselves for observation. Once the PLC has determined when and how the observation will take place, as well as what data will be recorded and by whom, the final step is to ensure all members are prepared to bring their data to the PLC meeting for discussion.

PROCESS OVERVIEW

The *Protocol for Discussing a Classroom Observation* follows a series of structured steps to facilitate meaningful reflection and actionable feedback. Below is an overview of each step.

Step 1: Determine Roles and Revisit Norms

The facilitator identifies and ensures everyone is clear about their roles, such as presenter, timekeeper, note-taker, and process observer. The facilitator also revisits norms as needed to set the stage for a productive discussion. This ensures that each participant understands their responsibilities, which supports a well-organized process.

Step 2: Review Focus of Observation

The facilitator reviews the focus for the observation with the team. This is often the type of feedback the teacher being observed requested the team focus on. This step ensures that all participants are aligned and understand the specific aspect of teaching being discussed, allowing for targeted feedback.

Step 3: Initial Reflection

In this step, the observed teacher briefly recaps and shares their reflections about the lesson. This reflection includes what went well and any challenges they faced, which sets the tone for a growth-oriented conversation and allows the team to understand the teacher's perspective before sharing their observations.

Step 4: Share Observations

Colleagues who observed the lesson silently review their notes and highlight factual observations—e.g., What did the students and teacher say and do related to the area of focus? All participants then take turns sharing their factual observations, focusing strictly on what they saw and heard, without interpretation or judgment. This step is critical for grounding the discussion in evidence-based reflections.

Step 5: Prepare Feedback

Next, teachers reflect on the factual observations and silently prepare to give their feedback. As they think and reflect, we encourage them to record and organize their feedback into the following three categories:

- *Praise*: Identify effective practices, strategies, and decisions and what made them effective. Use sentence starters like "I saw . . . ," "I noticed . . . ," or "One effective practice I saw was. . . ."
- *Probing Questions*: Encourage the teacher to think more deeply about their practice. Examples include, "I am curious to know more about . . . ," or "How did you decide . . . ?"
- *Polishing Suggestions*: Offer thoughtful suggestions to enhance instruction, using phrases like, "I wonder if you have considered . . . ," or "I am curious to know what might happen if . . . ." This approach helps maintain a supportive tone while encouraging growth.

Step 6: Share Praise of Effective Practice

Step 6 begins the feedback phase. Begin by having PLC members take turns sharing praise of effective practices and strategies observed. The facilitator encourages all members to share and ensures that responses to or comments about specific aspects of praise are held until later in the discussion. This step helps build confidence in the observed teacher and highlights strengths that can be leveraged in future lessons. The facilitator should also be mindful of how the feedback is given. We encourage them to be on the lookout for phrasing suggested by the sentence started in Step 5.

Step 7: Share Questions and Feedback

Participants now take turns asking probing questions and offering suggestions. The facilitator ensures that feedback remains supportive and that responses are held until the discussion step. As mentioned in Step 6, pay attention to how teachers articulate their feedback. It is important to ensure it is objective and kind. The sentence starters in Step 5 provide examples to help with this. This step encourages deep reflection and provides opportunities for instructional improvement.

Step 8: Discuss

Now that all the feedback is on the table, the facilitator leads a discussion about the praise, questions, and suggestions provided by the group. During this step, the observed teacher can begin by responding to the feedback, asking for clarification, or engaging in a dialogue that deepens their understanding about any of the feedback. A prompt that can get the conversation started could be, "What feedback just shared is most interesting and why?"

Step 9: Reflect

During the reflection step, the teacher who was observed shares their key thoughts and takeaways from the discussion. After the observed teacher has shared, the rest of the team shares their own takeaways, particularly ideas they plan to take back to their own classrooms. This step ensures that the learning is shared and that all participants benefit from the reflection.

Step 10: Next Steps

Step 10 involves outlining the next steps for the team, focusing on continuity and preparedness for future meetings. The facilitator should work with the team to clarify the agenda for the next meeting, including determining the protocol that will be used, identifying the materials or data that need to be gathered, and assigning roles and responsibilities to ensure accountability. In many cases, the PLC is engaging in a TLC. If this is the case, the next conversation should be focused on analyzing student work. It is important that participants share and clarify their next steps to maintain momentum and ensure everyone is prepared for the upcoming session.

Step 11: Debrief

Much like this step in other VITAL protocols, this step focuses on debriefing the observation discussion process. The debrief begins with the observed teacher sharing reflections about what aspects of the process were supportive of their learning. The facilitator then guides participants through a reflection, encouraging them to consider what supported their learning and what adjustments could be made to improve future sessions.

COMMON CHALLENGES AND SOLUTIONS

Throughout the discussion, certain challenges may arise. Below are common challenges and suggested ways to address them:

Feedback Feels Evaluative Rather Than Supportive

One common challenge is that feedback can sometimes feel evaluative, which may hinder open reflection. To address this, it is crucial to reinforce the use of depersonalized and nonjudgmental language and focus on specific evidence from the observation. For example, instead of saying, "The pacing of the lesson was too fast," an observer could say, "I noticed that several students seemed to struggle to keep up when you transitioned between activities quickly. How do you think adjusting the pacing might impact their understanding?" In addition, prior to giving feedback, it may be helpful to revisit any norms that might emphasize the importance of creating a safe space for feedback.

Dominance by One Voice in the Discussion

Another challenge is when one participant dominates the conversation, which can limit the input of others. Using a structured round-robin format ensures that all observers have an opportunity to contribute. Facilitators can also encourage quieter participants to talk by directly inviting them to share their insights. For example, "Alex, I'd love to hear your thoughts on the questioning strategies used." This approach, emphasized in the *Protocol for Establishing PLC Norms* (Chapter 8), ensures balanced participation and enriches the discussion.

Difficulty Focusing on the Agreed-Upon Aspect of the Lesson

Sometimes, discussions can veer off-topic or away from what the observed teacher has request, making it challenging to stay focused on the agreed-upon aspect of the lesson. A facilitator or timekeeper can gently redirect the conversation if it strays. Observers should also come prepared with notes that are specifically aligned to the focus area. For instance, if the focus is on differentiation, an observer might say, "I observed how you used different questions for groups at varying levels. How did you decide which questions to use for each group?" This keeps the discussion targeted and productive, following the structured approaches used in earlier protocols.

CONCLUSION

Reflecting on classroom practice through peer observations is a cornerstone of continuous professional growth and a core component of the feedback loops generated during the teaching and learning cycles in Phase 2 of VITAL Collaboration. As part of this feedback cycle, the *Protocol for Discussing a Classroom Observation* provides a safe, structured way to engage in meaningful dialogue that enhances instructional practice. By focusing on evidence, fostering trust, and supporting actionable next steps, this protocol helps sustain a culture of inquiry and continuous improvement, benefiting both teachers and their students. As an essential part of the teaching and learning cycles of VITAL Collaboration, this protocol ensures that reflective practice and feedback are consistently used to drive improvement. It also lays the groundwork for the final conversation in a teaching and learning cycle: analyzing student work. We explore this protocol next.

PROTOCOL FOR DISCUSSING A CLASSROOM OBSERVATION

Suggested Time: 60–90 Minutes
This protocol guides PLC teams through a process for observing and discussing a lesson in action. This protocol is designed to provide feedback of live instruction and prepares the team to analyze student work.

Step 1: Determine Roles and Revisit Norms (2 Minutes)

(1) The facilitator identifies and makes sure everyone is clear about their role—e.g., presenter, timekeeper, note-taker, and process observer.
(2) The facilitator revisits norms as needed.

Step 2: Review Focus of Observation (3 Minutes)

(1) The facilitator reviews the focus for the observation with the team.

Step 3: Initial Reflection (5–10 Minutes)

(1) The observed teacher briefly recaps and shares his or her reflections about the lesson.

Step 4: Share Observations (10 Minutes)

(1) Colleagues who observed the lesson silently review their notes and highlight factual observations: What did the students and teacher say and do related to the area of focus?
(2) All participants take turns sharing factual observations related to the focus area.

Step 5: Prepare Feedback (5 Minutes)

(1) Teachers reflect on the factual observations and silently prepare feedback. Consider the following types of feedback.
    (a) **Praise**—Focus on identifying effective practices, strategies, and decisions and what made them effective. Consider using sentence starters like "I saw . . . ," "I noticed . . . ," "I heard . . . ," or "One effective practice I saw was. . . ."
    (b) **Probing Questions**—Focus on questions that encourage the teacher to think about their practice more deeply. For example, "I am curious to know more about . . ." or "How did you decide . . . ?"

(c) **Suggestions**—Focus on thoughtful suggestions that could enhance the instruction. Make suggestions that respond to the teacher's focus for feedback. Possible sentence starters for polishing suggestions include the following: "I wonder if you have considered . . ." or "I am curious to know what might happen if. . . ."

Step 6: Share Praise of Effective Practice (5–10 Minutes)

(1) Participants take turns sharing praise for observations of effective practices and strategies observed.
(2) The facilitator should encourage all members to share and refrain from responding until Step 8.

Step 7: Share Questions and Feedback (5–10 Minutes)

(1) Participants take turns asking probing questions and offering suggestions.
(2) The facilitator should encourage all members to share and refrain from responding until Step 8.

Step 8: Discuss (15–20 Minutes)

(1) The facilitator leads a discussion about the praise, questions, and suggestions provided by the group.

Step 9: Reflect (5–10 Minutes)

(1) The teacher who was observed shares his or her thoughts and takeaways from the discussion.
(2) After the teacher has shared, the rest of the team shares their own takeaways from the discussion, particularly ideas they will take back to their own classroom.

Step 10: Next Steps (3–6 Minutes)

(1) The facilitator works with the team to outline the agenda for next meeting. If engaging in a TLC, often the next conversation is analyzing student work. Things to consider are the following:
   (a) What protocol will we use?
   (b) What preparation tasks need to happen in advance?
   (c) Who will be responsible for what?
(2) Participants clarify and share their next steps because of this meeting.

Step 11: Debrief (2–5 Minutes)

(1) Beginning with the observed teacher, participants share reflections about the process. Consider the following.
  (a) What supported your learning?
  (b) What could be adjusted next time to better support your learning?

CHAPTER 14

A Protocol for Analyzing Student Work

INTRODUCTION

In this chapter, we describe the final component of the teaching and learning cycle: analyzing student work. Analyzing student work is a cornerstone of effective teaching and a critical component of the teaching and learning cycle within Phase 2 of the VITAL Collaboration framework. This practice provides teachers with a window into student thinking and helps them to identify misconceptions, highlight areas of strength, and adapt their instruction to meet the diverse needs of their learners. When teachers engage in this reflective process collaboratively, they deepen their understanding of student learning and refine their instructional practice. By embedding the analysis of student work into their collaborative routine, PLCs create a continuous cycle of reflection and improvement, making it an essential part of ongoing professional learning.

PURPOSE

The purpose of the *Protocol for Analyzing Student Work* is to guide teacher teams through a structured process for reviewing student work products. By examining student responses to learning tasks, educators can uncover patterns, identify common misconceptions, and decide on the next steps for instruction. The insights gained from this analysis help to drive instructional decisions and help to ensure that teaching practices are both responsive and targeted to student needs. PLCs should use this protocol when they want to:

- Dive deeply into student thinking around specific concepts or skills.
- Assess the effectiveness of a particular instructional strategy.
- Plan targeted interventions to support student growth.

SUGGESTED TIME

Like most VITAL protocols, this protocol is designed to be completed in approximately 60–90 minutes, though teams may adjust the time based on the number and complexity of the student work samples they wish to analyze. When the work samples are complicated, or if there are many of them, it is recommended that teachers analyze a representative sample of student work rather than the complete set.

PREPARATION

Prior to the PLC meeting where student work will be analyzed, the facilitator should collaborate with the presenting teacher to gather a diverse range of student work samples that reflect varying levels of understanding. These samples should be directly connected to the team's instructional goals, the standards they are working toward, and/or a lesson previously tuned. If this protocol is taking place after a planned observation, the team should already have a plan for selecting the work to be examined. Additionally, the presenting teacher should develop a guiding question to focus the analysis. This question might address a specific concept, skill, or learning objective, such as, "What do these samples reveal about students' understanding of argument structure in persuasive writing?"

PROCESS OVERVIEW

The *Protocol for Analyzing Student Work* consists of eight steps, each building on the previous one to guide the team through a reflective and purposeful process. Below is an overview of each step.

Step 1: Determine Roles and Revisit Norms

Much like many of the other VITAL protocols, the facilitator begins the analysis of student work by ensuring each team member has a clear role to ensure the process runs smoothly. The facilitator should also take a few moments to revisit the group's working norms, such being open to different perspectives, and focusing on data and evidence. This helps sets the tone for a safe, focused, and productive analysis.

Step 2: Review the Focus Standard(s) and Analyze the Student Work Task

All team members should take time to individually review the focus standards related to the student work and engage with the task themselves as if they were a student. To do this, we encourage facilitators to suggest that PLC participants think through how they themselves would respond to the task or prompt. If it includes a short-response or yes/no questions, they can write down their answers. Putting themselves in the students' position and imagining their experience and perspective can give a deeper understanding of what the task demands.

Once everyone has worked on the task enough to feel confident in reviewing it, the team engages in a discussion about the task by addressing the following questions.

- How does the standard align with the student work task?
- What characteristics and features would define a high-quality, standard-aligned student response?
- What commonalities exist between the teacher work product and the student task?
- What potential misconceptions might students have about the task or any key concepts?

For example, in an analysis of student essays on persuasive writing, the team might identify that a high-quality response includes a clear argument, supporting evidence, logical reasoning, and a rebuttal. This shared understanding of what "good" looks like serves as a reference point for analyzing the student work.

Step 3: Pose Guiding Question to Focus Feedback and Present the Student Work Samples

The presenting teacher now introduces the student work samples and poses a guiding question that aligns with the team's instructional goals. This question will steer the analysis and feedback. For example, the presenter might ask, "How effectively are students using evidence to support their arguments in their essays?" The presenter then provides a brief overview of the context for the work samples, explaining why they chose these specific pieces and what they hope to learn from the analysis. Participants may ask clarifying questions to better understand the context, but these should be brief and focused on gaining clarity rather than probing deeply at this stage.

Step 4: Examine Artifacts

Next, the team silently reviews the student work samples, keeping the guiding question in mind. This period of quiet examination allows each member to observe the student work without the influence of others' perspectives. During this time, participants note specific evidence in the work that relates to the guiding question, such as how students are structuring their arguments or the types of evidence they are using.

After the silent review, the facilitator opens the floor for participants to share their observations. The focus here is on factual, evidence-based statements. For example, a participant might say, "I noticed that several students included a claim but did not provide specific examples to support their argument." This step sets the stage for a deeper analysis in the following steps.

Step 5: Respond to Student Work

In this step, the team shifts to discussing what the student work reveals about students' knowledge, skills, and thinking—particularly in relation to the standard(s). The facilitator guides the discussion with questions such as:

- What does the work show that students know and can do?
- To what extent is there evidence of mastery of the knowledge and skills related to the focus standards?

Keep in mind that the goal is to explore the implications of the observations and consider how they align with the team's instructional goals. For example, the team might identify that while students are formulating claims, they are not consistently backing them up with textual evidence. This insight suggests a need for ongoing instruction that emphasizes the importance of using evidence to support arguments.

Step 6: Determine Instructional Next Steps

The team then considers the implications of their analysis for the next steps in the instructional process. The facilitator prompts the group with questions like, "What do students need to move forward?" and "What instructional strategies might support students' continued growth?" From this, the team collaboratively identifies specific actions to take in future lessons. For instance, they might decide to implement a minilesson on how to incorporate evidence into arguments, followed by guided practice activities. The facilitator should work to ensure that these next steps are actionable, focused, and aligned with the team's overall goals.

Step 7: Plan for Next Meeting

As always, before closing the session the facilitator works with the team to outline the agenda for their next meeting. Since this protocol often concludes a teaching and learning cycle, it is important to decide if the team will now start a new round or move into Phase 3 of VITAL Collaboration. Based on what the team decides, the group should discuss what protocol they will use, what preparation tasks need to be completed in advance, and who will be responsible for each.

Step 8: Debrief the Process

In the final step, the team reflects on the process itself. Beginning with the presenting teacher, each participant shares their thoughts on what supported their learning during the session and what could be adjusted for next time. The facilitator might ask, "How did our analysis today help us better understand student learning?" or "What could we change in our process to improve our next analysis of student work?" This reflection helps the team refine their collaborative practices and continually improve the protocol's effectiveness.

COMMON CHALLENGES AND SOLUTIONS

Several challenges often arise during the analysis of student work. By anticipating these obstacles and employing targeted solutions, facilitators can help their PLCs enhance the quality and impact of their discussions.

Hyper-Focusing

One common challenge PLCs experience when analyzing student work is the inclination to focus on individual student performance rather than identifying broader trends. Teachers may find it difficult to shift their attention from specific student errors to the patterns present across multiple work samples. To address this, the facilitator can reframe the discussion with prompts such as, "What are we noticing across most of these samples?" This approach helps the team focus on collective insights, leading to more generalizable and actionable instructional strategies.

Deficit Mindsets

Another challenge is the tendency to overlook students' strengths and concentrate solely on their weaknesses. When discussions become deficit-focused, the team may miss valuable opportunities to build on what students are already doing well. Facilitators can introduce a strengths-based lens by first asking participants to identify what students did effectively. For example, the facilitator might say, "Let's start by highlighting one thing each student did well in their responses." This practice fosters a balanced dialogue and helps the team approach areas for growth with a positive mindset.

Being Too Evaluative

A third challenge is that discussions may become overly evaluative rather than exploratory. When the focus shifts to judging student work as simply "correct" or "incorrect," the conversation may lose its depth. The facilitator can redirect this by encouraging descriptive language and evidence-based observations. For instance, instead of stating, "This student didn't follow the instructions," a more productive approach would be, "This student identified a main idea but did not provide supporting details." This type of analysis invites exploration into students' thinking processes and instructional implications.

Lack of Time

As is often the case, time constraints often present another challenge, particularly when teams attempt to analyze every aspect of student work. To manage this, the facilitator should guide the team to prioritize specific aspects of the work that align with their current instructional focus. For example, if the team's goal is to enhance students' use of evidence in writing, they might concentrate their analysis solely on this aspect. By narrowing the scope, the team can delve more deeply into the most relevant areas and develop targeted instructional responses.

CONCLUSION

Analyzing student work is a powerful practice that empowers educators to reflect on their students' learning and adapt their instructional approaches. When embedded into regular collaborative routines, it becomes a central component of data-driven decision-making and professional growth within the PLC. By engaging in this structured protocol, teacher teams not only gain insights into student understanding but also collaboratively develop strategies to enhance their teaching practices.

As you implement this protocol, consider how it complements other practices discussed in previous chapters, such as lesson tuning and setting data-based learning goals. Together, these practices form a cohesive approach to improving teaching and learning within the VITAL Collaboration framework. By regularly analyzing student work, teams can create a cycle of continuous reflection and growth that leads to improved student outcomes.

PREP SHEET FOR ANALYZING STUDENT WORK

Presenting Teacher:
Content / Grade:

Directions

This sheet is designed to help teachers prepare to engage in collaboratively analyzing student work. To help optimize the analysis, presenting teachers are encouraged to do the following.

(1) Analyze the focus standard(s) of the lesson from which the student work was generated in advance by using the *Analyzing Standards Note-taking Tool*. This should ideally be done in a previous PLC meeting.
(2) Respond to the prompts below. They are designed to help presenting teachers prepare for the student work analysis.
(3) Share everything in advance with your PLC colleagues in advance of the PLC meeting or have everything ready to share at the beginning of the meeting.

Preparation Prompts

- Briefly describe the student work task.
- What is your guiding question to focus the analysis and feedback of the student work?
- Are there key things to know about the student work or the lesson from which they came?

What to Share in Advance

- Completed prep sheet
- Copies of a blank student work task
- Student work to analyze. This can be a representative sample from the class or selected samples that align with the guiding question. Some teachers also like to make copies and redact student names.

PROTOCOL FOR ANALYZING STUDENT WORK

Suggested Time: 60–90 Minutes

This protocol guides PLC teams through a process for analyzing student work. It is designed to bring closure to a teaching and learning cycle. After this protocol, teams decide to engage in a new TLC or spend time reviewing their progress.

Step 1: Determine Roles and Revisit Norms (3 Minutes)

(1) The facilitator identifies and makes sure everyone is clear about their role—e.g., presenter, timekeeper, note-taker, and process observer.
(2) The facilitator revisits norms as needed.

Step 2: Review the Focus Standard(s) and Analyze the Student Work Task (10–25 Minutes)

(1) All members review the standard(s) and individually complete the student work task.
(2) Discuss as a team the following:
  (a) How the standard aligns to the student work task.
  (b) Commonalities of the teacher work product to the student task.
  (c) The characteristics and features of a high-quality, standard-aligned student work product.
  (d) Predictions about possible student misconceptions.

Step 3: Pose Guiding Question to Focus Feedback and Present Student Work Task Samples (5–10 Minutes)

(1) The presenting teacher does the following:
  (a) Poses a guiding question to direct the analysis and feedback that aligns to the PLC goal.
  (b) Briefly shares and describes the purpose for choosing the student work samples.
(2) Participants ask clarifying questions. These should be short questions intended to clarify, not probe.

Step 4: Examine Artifacts (10–15 Minutes)

(1) Participants silently review the student work.
(2) Participants share factual observations about the student work related to the guiding question.

(3) Participants discuss the following.
   (a) What is the work showing students know and can do?
   (b) To what extent is there evidence of mastery of the knowledge and skills as they relate to the focus standards?

Step 5: Respond to Student Work (10–15 Minutes)

(1) What are the implications for the next steps in the instructional process? What do students need to move forward?
(2) What instructional next step might support students' continued growth?

Step 6: Feedback and Reflection (5–10 Minutes)

(1) Presenters reflect on the discussion and share instructional next steps.
(2) Participants share takeaways.

Step 7: Next Steps (2–6 Minutes)

(3) The facilitator works with the team to outline the agenda for next meeting. Things to consider are the following.
   (a) Are we beginning a new teacher and learning cycle?
   (b) What preparation tasks need to happen in advance?
   (c) Who will be responsible for what?
(4) Participants clarify and share their next steps as a result of this meeting.

Step 8: Debrief (2–6 Minutes)

(2) Beginning with the presenting teacher, participants share reflections about the process. Consider the following.
   (a) What supported your learning?
   (b) What could be adjusted next time to better support our learning?

CHAPTER 15

A Protocol for Monitoring Progress of Teaching and Learning

INTRODUCTION

Monitoring progress toward teaching and learning goals is a crucial aspect of the continuous improvement cycle within the VITAL Collaboration framework. This chapter focuses on Phase 3, where educators review their progress toward the goals established during Phase 1. By monitoring their progress, teacher teams can ensure that their efforts remain aligned with student needs and the team's instructional objectives.

In previous chapters, we discussed the importance of setting SMART goals for teaching improvement and learning outcomes. For instance, a team might set a goal to increase the percentage of students achieving proficiency in writing argumentative essays from 60% to 80% by the end of the semester. This chapter builds on that foundation by providing a structured protocol for monitoring progress toward those goals, allowing educators to assess the effectiveness of their teaching strategies and make informed decisions based on data. Through this reflective practice, teams can identify successes, address challenges, and adjust their approaches to better support student learning.

PURPOSE

The purpose of this protocol is to provide a systematic approach for teacher teams to determine where they are in the process of working toward their goals. By regularly reviewing student data and teaching artifacts, educators can identify areas of strength, recognize challenges, and make data-informed decisions to enhance their effectiveness. This monitoring process not only helps teams stay focused on their goals but also fosters a sense of collective responsibility for student outcomes.

SUGGESTED TIME

The protocol is designed to be completed in approximately 60–90 minutes, though this time may be adjusted based on the specific goals being monitored and the data available for review.

PREPARATION

Prior to the meeting, the facilitator should gather relevant student data, including assessment results, formative data, and any additional evidence that reflects student progress toward the established goals. For instance, if the team is monitoring progress in reading comprehension, they might collect data from recent quizzes, standardized tests, and classroom assessments.

Team members should also review the SMART goals set during Phase 1, ensuring that everyone is clear on the expectations for monitoring progress. In this case, if the goal is to improve student performance in a specific reading level, teachers might revisit baseline data, such as initial reading assessments.

In addition to gathering data, the facilitator should prepare a set of guiding questions to help focus the analysis. These questions might include:

- What does the data tell us about student progress toward the goals?
- Which instructional strategies have been most effective in supporting this progress?
- What challenges have arisen, and how can we address them?

Finally, the facilitator should ensure that the norms for collaborative discussion are clear, emphasizing a growth mindset and the importance of constructive feedback.

PROCESS OVERVIEW

The protocol for monitoring progress consists of nine key steps that guide the team through a structured review of their teaching and learning goals.

Step 1: Determine Roles and Revisit Norms

The facilitator begins by assigning roles to each team member to ensure the process runs smoothly. Common roles include presenter, timekeeper, notetaker, and process observer. As usual, the facilitator should revisit the group's norms. This brief step sets the tone for a safe, focused, and productive monitoring process.

Step 2: Review the PLC's Teaching Improvement Goal

In this step, the team quickly reviews the SMART goals they established for improving teaching and learning, along with any baseline data that was previously collected. For example, if the team's goal was to enhance students' analytical writing skills, they would revisit the specific metrics set, such as achieving a certain percentage of students scoring at or above the proficiency level on writing assessments.

Step 3: Review Data Reports and Teaching Artifacts

Next, the team reviews any data provided, such as data reports and relevant teaching artifacts. Participants should ensure that all team members can access the materials for the session. They begin by silently reviewing the data, such as recent assessment results, and then the teaching artifacts, such as work samples. For instance, a teacher might bring in a rubric used to assess argumentative essays to discuss whether the strategies aligned with the SMART goals are being effectively implemented. After this silent review, the team discusses any clarifying questions regarding the data, ensuring that everyone has a clear understanding of the information presented.

Step 4: Examine Data

The team silently reviews the data again, this time focusing on factual observations. Participants should note specific findings, such as:

- "15 students are proficient at identifying main arguments in texts."
- "10 students are not in jeopardy for meeting the reading comprehension benchmark."
- "The class average is lowest for essay structure, with a score of 68%."
- "The class average is highest for thesis statements, with a score of 85%."

Once all observations are made, each team member shares their factual observations regarding the student data. This collaborative sharing continues until all relevant insights have been discussed, creating a comprehensive overview of student progress.

Step 5: Examine and Discuss Teaching Artifacts

Following the data analysis, team members turn their attention to the teaching artifacts related to the SMART goals. Each participant silently reviews these artifacts, making factual observations about the teaching practices implemented. For instance, they might note:

- "We taught five lessons using the 'Claim, Evidence, Reasoning' instructional strategy."
- "Four classrooms implemented the same instructional strategy during their writing units."
- "We tried graphic organizers, peer reviews, and modeling techniques related to our teaching improvement goal."

Each team member then shares their observations, continuing until all relevant insights have been shared.

Step 6: Infer and Question

During this discussion phase, the team explores tentative conclusions and interpretations based on their observations from the data and artifacts. They address guiding questions, such as:

- "What conclusions might we draw from the data?"
- "What evidence do we have of student mastery or struggles?"
- "What instructional strategies have positively impacted student learning?"

The facilitator can prompt participants to think critically about their findings by suggesting tentative conclusions, such as:

- "The data suggest that students have mastered the skill of developing strong thesis statements."
- "Most students are struggling with essay structure, indicating a need for additional instruction in this area."
- "As teachers, we need more practice with providing effective feedback on student drafts."

This reflective discussion encourages deeper inquiry into the implications of the observations made.

Step 7: Review and Revise PLC SMART Goal

With insights gathered from the discussion, the team revisits their SMART goal for improving teaching. Based on the analysis, they determine whether to keep the goal as is, make small adjustments, or rewrite it entirely. For example, if the data shows significant improvement in thesis statements but struggles with overall essay structure, the team might adjust their goal to focus specifically on enhancing essay organization skills. They discuss what data is needed to set the new goal and establish a timeline for revisiting the goals.

Step 8: Next Steps

The facilitator works with the team to outline the agenda for the next meeting. For example, the team may decide to engage in a couple more TLCs, or they may decide to move into Phase 4 and share their results with the broader school community. Based on their decisions, the team should then discuss what protocols will be used, what preparation tasks need to happen in advance, and who will be responsible for each task. For instance, they might agree that one member will identify a standard to analyze at the next meeting. Participants should clarify and share their next steps to ensure accountability.

Step 9: Debrief

To conclude the session, participants reflect on the monitoring process. Starting with the presenting teacher, each member shares their thoughts on what supported their learning during the session and what could be adjusted in future meetings to better enhance the collaborative process. For example, a teacher might suggest, "I found the structured observations really helpful, but I'd like to have more time for the infer and question phase next time." This reflection helps solidify the learning from the meeting and reinforces a culture of continuous improvement.

COMMON CHALLENGES AND SOLUTIONS

As teams engage in monitoring progress, several common challenges may arise. By anticipating these obstacles and developing strategies to address them, teams can enhance the effectiveness of their discussions.

Difficulty Analyzing Data

One challenge is the difficulty in interpreting data accurately, especially when educators have varying levels of experience with data analysis. For example, a teacher may feel overwhelmed by assessment results presented in a spreadsheet. To combat this, facilitators can provide professional development opportunities focused on data literacy, ensuring all team members feel equipped to engage with data effectively. Additionally, using visual aids, such as charts or graphs that summarize data trends, can help clarify complex information.

Maintaining Focus

Another common issue is maintaining focus during discussions. Teams may struggle to stay on topic; conversations can drift into unrelated areas. The facilitator should keep the conversation aligned with established goals and guiding questions, reminding team members to consider collective insights rather than individual cases. Setting clear norms about staying on topic can foster a more productive discussion. For instance, the facilitator might use a visual timer to indicate time allocated for each step, helping the team stay focused.

Resistance to Change

Resistance to change can also hinder progress, particularly if previous instructional practices have become entrenched. For example, a teacher might be reluctant to abandon a long-used strategy, even if data suggests it's not effective. Facilitators should create a supportive environment where team members feel comfortable sharing their concerns. Emphasizing the shared goal of improving student outcomes and celebrating small successes can help build a collective commitment to change. For instance, highlighting a case where a new instructional strategy led to noticeable improvement in student engagement can motivate the team to embrace new practices.

Time Constraints

Time constraints can limit the depth of analysis and discussion. Teams may feel pressured to rush through data reviews, leading to superficial conclusions. Facilitators can mitigate this by scheduling the progress monitoring across multiple PLC meetings. Additionally, considering alternative meeting times or adjusting the schedule to accommodate monitoring discussions can help ensure this critical work receives the attention it deserves. For example, if teams meet weekly, dedicating the first meeting of each month exclusively to monitoring progress can allow for more in-depth exploration without the usual time constraints.

CONCLUSION

Monitoring progress toward teaching and learning goals is an essential practice that empowers educators to reflect on their teaching effectiveness and adapt their strategies to better meet the needs of their students. By embedding this protocol into their regular collaborative routines, PLCs can create a culture of continuous improvement, ensuring that their efforts remain aligned with student needs and instructional objectives.

As you prepare to implement this protocol, consider how it connects with the previous protocols discussed in this book, particularly those that are part of a teaching and learning cycle in Phase 2. Together, these practices form a comprehensive approach to enhancing teaching and learning within the VITAL Collaboration framework. In the next chapter, we will share a protocol for sharing and celebrating progress with the broader school community.

PROTOCOL FOR MONITORING PROGRESS OF TEACHING AND LEARNING

Suggested Time: 60–90 Minutes

This protocol guides PLC teams through a process for reviewing a PLC's progress toward the student learning and teaching improvement goals. This protocol is designed to provide feedback on live instruction and prepares the team to analyze student work.

Step 1: Determine Roles and Revisit Norms (3 Minutes)

(1) The facilitator identifies and makes sure everyone is clear about their role—e.g., presenter, timekeeper, note-taker, and process observer.
(2) The facilitator revisits norms as needed.

Step 2: Review the PLC's Teaching Improvement Goal (5 Minutes)

(1) Review the team's SMART Goals for improving teaching and learning, along with any baseline data.

Step 3: Review Data Reports and Teaching Artifacts (5–10 Minutes)

(1) Review data and teaching artifacts by doing the following:
    (a) Ensure all participants can access data reports and teaching artifacts.
    (b) Silently review data.
    (c) Silently review teaching artifacts.
(2) Discuss any clarifying questions about the data reports.

Step 4: Examine Data (10–15 Minutes)

(1) Silently review data again, this time, make note of factual observations. Consider the examples below.
    (a) ___ no. of students are proficient at . . .
    (b) ___ no. of students are not in warning for . . .
    (c) The class average is lowest for . . .
    (d) The class average is highest for . . .
(2) Each team member shares factual observations about the student data. Continue until all relevant observations have been shared.

Step 5: Examine and Discuss Teaching Artifacts (5–10 Minutes)

(1) Silently review artifacts of teaching practice related to the SMART goal.
(2) Make note of factual observations. Consider the following examples.
  (a) ___ no. of times we taught lessons with ___ instructional strategy.
  (b) ___ no. of classrooms that implemented ___ instructional strategy.
  (c) We tried ___, ____, and ____ related to our teaching improvement goal.
(3) Each team member shares factual observations about the teaching artifacts. Continue until all relevant observations have been shared.

Step 6: Infer and Question (10–15 Minutes)

(1) Discuss the following questions:
  (a) What tentative conclusions/interpretations might we draw from the observations noticed in the data? Below are examples and sentence starters for possible conclusions:
    (i) The data suggest . . .
    (ii) The students have mastered . . .
    (iii) Most students are struggling with . . .
    (iv) Students need more practice with . . .
    (v) As teachers, we need more practice with . . .
    (vi) I think that ___ instructional strategy has impacted students by ____.
    (vii) Data suggest . . . because . . . a possible reason is . . .
    (viii) What, if any, new questions are we asking?
    (ix) What, if any, additional data do we need to collect and analyze?

Step 7: Review and Revise PLC SMART Goal (10–15 Minutes)

(1) Review the team's SMART Goal for improving teaching. Based on the analysis, determine if the team needs to keep, adjust, or rewrite its goal. Consider the following.
  (a) Keep goal as is and continue to work toward it.
  (b) Adjust: make small adjustments to goal in the moment.
  (c) Set new goal: Determine what data is needed to set the new goal and set date/time to conduct the Protocol for Setting Student Learning Goals (Phase 1).

Step 8: Next Steps (2–6 Minutes)

(1) The facilitator works with the team to outline the agenda for next meeting. Things to consider are the following.
   (a) What protocol will we use?
   (b) What preparation tasks need to happen in advance?
   (c) Who will be responsible for what?
(2) Participants clarify and share their next steps as a result of this meeting.

Step 9: Debrief (3–6 Minutes)

(3) Beginning with the presenting teacher, participants share reflections about the process. Consider the following.
   (a) What supported your learning?
   (b) What could be adjusted next time to better support our learning?

CHAPTER 16

A Protocol for Sharing and Celebrating Learning

INTRODUCTION

The final phase of the VITAL Collaboration process culminates in a powerful opportunity for PLCs to share and celebrate their learning experiences with other PLCs in their school as a networked improvement community. This chapter introduces the *Protocol for Sharing and Celebrating Learning*, which serves as the anchor for Phase 4. This protocol proposes a structured way for schools to bring closure to the teaching and learning cycles by enabling PLCs to share their insights, successes, and challenges with the broader school community. It is important to point out this protocol suggests just one way PLCs can share and celebrate together as a school. As with all of the protocols, the emphasis is not on the protocol itself, but the intent behind it.

PURPOSE

As mentioned above, the *Protocol for Sharing and Celebrating Learning* supports Phase 4 of VITAL Collaboration by bringing closure to all four phases of VITAL. It also serves as a transition to a new cycle of collaborative learning. Many schools have PLCs engage in all four phases of VITAL over a semester and begin a new round the following semester. This protocol is best used in a schoolwide context after multiple PLCs have engaged in their VITAL journeys and are ready to share their learning.

SUGGESTED TIME

On average, this protocol can take 90–120 minutes, depending on the number of PLCs sharing. If there is limited time available or if the number of PLCs sharing is large, it may be necessary to schedule multiple sharing sessions.

PREPARATION

Before the public sharing, a school leader should communicate the purpose of the meeting, highlighting the importance of celebrating teacher and student growth. PLC facilitators can meet together to plan the sharing and celebration. Each PLC team should also be given time to prepare a brief presentation (approximately 10 minutes) that shares key aspects of their VITAL journey, including their goals, challenges encountered, strategies implemented, and outcomes achieved. Teams may use visuals, artifacts, or other materials to illustrate their experiences. For example, a team could create a slideshow showcasing before-and-after examples of student work or a short video capturing moments from their collaborative efforts. A shared document or presentation platform can be set up for teams to display their work during the session, such as a shared Google workspace.

PROCESS OVERVIEW

The *Protocol for Sharing and Celebrating Learning* consists of four key steps: reviewing the purpose, sharing learning by each PLC, group reflection, and debriefing the process. Each is described below.

Step 1: Review Purpose and Set Norms

The school leader sets the tone by emphasizing the significance of celebrating both student and teacher growth. This step helps to frame the session as an opportunity for collective learning, encouraging participants to listen with intent as each PLC shares their VITAL journey. For instance, the school leader might say, "As we listen to each team today, let's focus on identifying one key takeaway or question to learn more about their journey." In addition to clarifying the purpose, time should be dedicated to setting some norms for the event. This can be done by having teams share their favorite norms. A note-taker should be assigned to record these for everyone to see.

Step 2: Share Learning by PLC

The next step consists of PLCs taking turns sharing their learning, with opportunities for questions and discussion. To do this, each PLC team presents their journey, using visuals or artifacts to illustrate key moments in their collaborative work. One team may choose to showcase a student's growth in reading fluency, displaying a graph that highlights progress over time and sharing strategies they used to achieve this outcome. Another team might present a short video of a classroom activity that transformed student engagement in math, explaining the steps they took to design and implement the lesson.

During the presentations, participants should be encouraged to listen for teaching connections and to pose questions. For example, colleagues might ask, "How did you address the diverse needs of students during this process?" After each presentation, the group shares insights and celebrates the team's success with a round of applause or a spirit chant. This process is repeated for each PLC team, creating a positive atmosphere that honors the hard work and achievements of all participants.

Step 3: Group Reflection

Following the presentations, PLCs convene separately to discuss the patterns and trends noticed across teams. They explore how the collective learning can be leveraged for future actions at the team or school level. For instance, one group might note, "Several teams found success using student self-assessment tools. How might we incorporate this practice schoolwide?" After this internal discussion, the teams come back together to shares their ideas with the larger group, fostering a sense of unity and shared purpose. An example outcome from this step might include a plan to host cross-PLC sessions where teams exchange resources and strategies, or they may decide to implement a schoolwide initiative for enhancing formative assessment practices.

Step 4: Debrief the Process

The session concludes with a reflection on the sharing and celebration process itself. Participants discuss what made the discussion productive and identify potential improvements for future sessions. For instance, a participant might say, "I appreciated the use of visuals in the presentations; it really helped me understand the strategies used. Next time, perhaps we could include a brief Q&A segment after each presentation to dive deeper into the specifics." This step not only reinforces the collaborative culture but also models the reflective practice central to VITAL Collaboration. By continuously refining the process, schools can ensure that these sharing sessions remain meaningful and impactful.

COMMON CHALLENGES AND SOLUTIONS

Lengthy Presentations

This protocol encourages the PLC presentations to be brief. Despite this, it is not uncommon for presentations to run long. Understanding this, there are two reasons we encourage brevity. First, the intent of having PLCs present is not to share every aspect of their inquiry and learning, but rather to provide enough information to pique the interest of colleagues so conversations continue after the meeting. The hope is that teachers listening to a presentation will want to learn more and reach out to their colleagues later, and in doing so, continue to foster a culture of learning and sharing. The second reason is that preparing for a 10-minute presentation is doable. We find that presentations longer than this can be stressful and very time-consuming to plan for.

Limited Participation

Another challenge is that some participants may be hesitant to share or engage fully during the celebration process. To address this, school leaders can establish clear norms that promote inclusivity, such as encouraging every voice to be heard. One way to do this is to have PLCs take turns sharing a norm they use in their own meetings. A strategy to encourage participation is to use a round-robin format during reflections, where each participant shares one insight or question. Creating a supportive environment where all contributions are valued can help to build confidence and engagement among participants.

Another reasons a PLC may be hesitant to share is that they may not have made as much progress as they would have hoped for. If this is the case, leaders should to remind teams that we learn just as much, if not more, from attempts to improve that are not as successful as we desire as from triumphs. Even if teams did not see the growth they wanted, there is still much to learn from their attempts. Thus, it is important to create a culture that embraces and celebrates attempts to try new ideas, even when they may not pan out.

Staying Focused on Learning

It is not uncommon for the celebratory nature of the protocol to lead to conversations that veer off-topic. Facilitators can mitigate this by using prompts that keep the focus on teaching and learning. For example, after each presentation, the person facilitating the meeting might ask, "What specific strategy shared by this team could be adapted to your classroom?" This question helps guide the discussion back to practical applications and shared learning.

Managing Time

With multiple PLCs sharing, time management can become a challenge. Facilitators should communicate the time limits for each presentation and use visual cues or a timer to keep the session on track. For example, a bell or a visual countdown timer can signal when it's time to wrap up a segment. Building in flexibility allows adjustments as needed without losing the overall flow of the process.

CONCLUSION

The *Protocol for Sharing and Celebrating Learning* provides a meaningful closure to the VITAL process. By sharing their journeys, PLCs function as a networked improvement community in their school, and in doing so, reinforce the collective commitment to growth and improvement. This protocol not only celebrates individual and group accomplishments but also sets the stage for ongoing collaborative efforts. Through reflection and sharing, the school community continues to build on its collective knowledge, ready to embark on the next cycle of VITAL Collaboration.

PROTOCOL FOR SHARING AND CELEBRATING LEARNING

Suggested Time: 90–120 Minutes
This protocol guides PLC teams through a process for observing and discussing a lesson in action. This protocol is designed to provide feedback of live instruction and prepares the team to analyze student work.

Step 1: Review Purpose and Set Norms (5 Minutes)

1) A school leader sets the tone for celebrating student and teacher growth by clarifying the purpose of the gathering.
2) The school leader asks teams to share and recommend norms for the celebration.
3) A note-taker records the norms on a white board or chart paper.

Step 2: Share Learning by PLC (10 Minutes Each Team)

PLC teams take turns doing the following:

(1) The PLC facilitator or other representative presents and shares their team's VITAL journey of student and teacher learning with the whole group using what they have prepared.
(2) Colleagues from other PLCs listen for teaching connections and ask questions to learn more.
(3) After the presentation, the whole group does the following.
    (i) Take turns sharing insights and questions
    (ii) Determines a fun way to cheer on the PLC team's success. Here are a few ideas:
        (1) Firecracker: Slap hands together in an upward motion and snap several times
        (2) Round of applause: Clap continuously in a circular motion
        (3) Play a segment of a favorite song
        (4) Spirit call: Come up with a fun chant for the success of the team
(4) Repeat this process for each PLC team.

Step 3: Group Reflection (20 Minutes)

(1) After all groups have presented and have been celebrated, PLCs reconvene to discuss the following.
    (a) What patterns and trends did they notice across teams?
    (b) What actions might teams or the school make to leverage the school's collective learning?

(2) Once PLCs have had time to discuss, teams share and discuss their ideas as a whole group.

Step 4: Debrief the Process (10 Minutes)

(1) Have individuals share reflections and takeaways about the celebration and sharing process. Discuss the following:
   (a) What helped the discussion be productive?
   (b) What could be done next time to make it even more productive?

Part IV

MORE TOOLS AND IDEAS

Part IV offers a collection of additional tools and ideas that build on the concepts and practices introduced in earlier sections of the book. These chapters provide facilitators and their teams with additional information and strategies that can be used to prepare for or deepen their collaborative work.

Chapter 17, "Getting Started With VITAL Collaboration," offers guidance for PLC facilitators or teacher leaders who are starting or rebooting their PLCs with a focus on VITAL Collaboration. The chapter suggests a handful of strategies facilitators can use to build their capacity to lead their PLC. These strategies include engaging in a collective self-assessment and reflection as a team, reading sections of this book together as a team, making a schedule for all PLC meetings, and creating a professional learning community for facilitators. Together these strategies will set PLCs up for success when engaging in VITAL for the first time.

Chapter 18, "Crafting SMART Goals for PLCs," provides guidance on creating specific, measurable, achievable, relevant, and time-bound goals. This chapter builds on the goal-setting protocols in Part III, offering a deeper exploration of what makes a goal effective. By understanding how to craft SMART goals, teams can set clear targets that drive their work and monitor progress more effectively.

Chapter 19, "Why Standards are Difficult to Understand," addresses the complexities of learning standards, offering insights into common challenges teachers face when interpreting them. This chapter complements the *Protocol for Analyzing Standards* in Part III, providing a deeper understanding of why standards can be tricky and how to approach them collaboratively. By unpacking these complexities, teams can ensure their instruction is aligned with the standards and meets students' learning needs.

In sum, the readings in Part IV serve as valuable extensions of the practices explored in earlier chapters. By engaging with these topics, PLCs can enhance their collaborative efforts, refine their instructional approaches, and continue building their capacity to implement the VITAL Collaboration framework effectively.

CHAPTER 17

Getting Started With VITAL Collaboration

INTRODUCTION

This chapter is designed for PLC facilitators or teacher leaders who are either leading PLCs for the first time or rebooting how their PLCs function in preparation for engaging in VITAL Collaboration. Both scenarios require you to embark on a new path. It can feel overwhelming to prepare your PLC for engaging in VITAL Collaboration, but having a clear plan and tools in place makes a world of difference. This chapter provides suggestions and tools for preparing to launch a successful VITAL PLC, from assessing your current starting point to creating a structured schedule that encourages productive collaboration.

REFLECT ON CURRENT PLC PRACTICES

Before fully diving into all four phases of VITAL Collaboration, it may be beneficial to begin with a simple needs-sensing process. A key part of this process is conducting a self-assessment or engaging in collective reflection at the team level. This will help identify your team's current strengths and areas for improvement. On page 185, you will find a simple tool that PLCs can use to assess existing practices. This tool focuses on some of the core management functions of a PLC described in Chapter 4.

Using the Self-Assessment of Collaborative Practices, and analyzing the data it gathers, can help PLC facilitators and their teams create a more targeted approach to improvement. By reflecting on specific practices that impact the effectiveness of PLC meetings, facilitators and team members can highlight areas where they excel and pinpoint opportunities for growth. For instance, if the reflection reveals that meetings often lack a clear agenda, the team can prioritize consistently developing and using detailed agendas to ensure focused discussions. Similarly, if members indicate that norms are not consistently reviewed at the start of meetings, the facilitator might introduce a routine to revisit norms at the beginning of each session. In short, this process helps build a shared understanding of the PLC's current state, providing a baseline from which progress can be measured. The self-assessment data can guide decision-making, helping facilitators and teams set clear goals directly aligned with their needs.

The self-assessment process also encourages collective ownership of a PLC's development. By involving all team members in the assessment, the group builds a shared accountability for improving practices. For example, if the assessment highlights that the team rarely reflects on meeting processes or key learning moments, members can decide collectively to dedicate the last 10 minutes of each meeting to reflect on what went well and what could be improved. The results provide a focus for ongoing conversations, enabling the team to prioritize changes that will have the most significant impact on their collaborative work. As a result, the PLC can engage more effectively in VITAL Collaboration by ensuring foundational elements, such as meeting structure, role clarity, and productive dialogue, are in place before moving on to more rigorous work aimed at improving instructional practice.

Self-Assessment of Collaborative Practices

This tool enables a self-assessment that PLCs can use to strengthen the efficiency of their collaborative practices. To use this tool, have team members complete the assessment separately. Afterwards, share and discuss the results as a team to identify areas to target for improvement.

PLC Practices	Always	Often	Sometimes	Never
Have a clear **agenda** for every PLC meeting.	-	-	-	-
Prepare and review necessary **materials** in advance.	-	-	-	-
Establish **roles** and review **norms** at the beginning of every conversation.	-	-	-	-
Clarify the **purpose** of the meeting at the outset.	-	-	-	-
Use organized **processes** to structure conversation, inquiry, and analysis.	-	-	-	-
Identify, share, and discuss examples of **professional practice**.	-	-	-	-
Use **standards** to frame and drive conversation and analysis of practice.	-	-	-	-
Provide thoughtful **feedback** about professional practices.	-	-	-	-
Reflect on meeting processes and what was learned.	-	-	-	-
Set **next agenda** for the following meeting before adjourning.	-	-	-	-

ENGAGE IN A VITAL COLLABORATION BOOK STUDY

Another strategy PLCs can use to build their readiness for VITAL Collaboration is to engage in a book study of this text as a team. To conduct a book study, have PLC members read specific chapters or Parts I and II of this book. Encourage them to record responses to any pre-reading and post-reading prompts; these responses can then spur discussion during PLC meetings. A helpful approach for fostering conversation about assigned readings is to use a text-based discussion protocol, such as the text-rendering protocol (National School Reform Faculty, n.d.). This protocol encourages participants to engage deeply with a reading while focusing on parts that resonate with them the most. Below is a simplified version of this protocol.

Text-Rendering Protocol

1. **Select Key Passages**: Each PLC member reads a designated chapter or section of the book and selects a *phrase*, a *sentence*, and a *word* that they find meaningful, impactful, or thought-provoking. For longer readings, the text should be read in advance. For shorter readings, the reading can be done quietly together during a meeting.
2. **Share and Discuss**: After participants have read, they engage in three rounds of sharing. After everyone has shared during each round, the team should discuss what they noticed during the sharing.
    - **Round 1**: Each participant shares their chosen **phrase** with the group, briefly explaining why it stood out to them.
    - **Round 2**: Each member then shares their **sentence**, discussing its significance in the context of their teaching practice or the collaborative work they will undertake.
    - **Round 3**: Finally, each person shares their selected **word**, explaining how it captures an essential concept or idea from the text.
3. **Discuss**: After all rounds have been completed, the group reflects on the discussion as a whole. What themes emerged? How do these concepts connect to the goals of VITAL Collaboration?

PRACTICE USING THE PROTOCOLS

Another strategy that helps PLCs prepare for VITAL Collaboration is practicing some of the protocols before diving into all phases of the framework. To get teams comfortable with using VITAL protocols, start with either the Protocol for Analyzing Standards, the Protocol for Tuning a Lesson, or the Protocol for Analyzing Student Work. Each of these protocols is powerful on its own for improving teaching practice, but their impact is amplified when used together as part of a teaching and learning cycle, aligned with a teaching improvement goal.

MAKE A SCHEDULE

Many first-time VITAL PLC facilitators find it very helpful to map out or create a schedule of their meetings in advance. On the following pages is a simple organizer that can be used for this purpose. The tool has three sections, one each for the first three phases of VITAL Collaboration. In the first section, PLC facilitators are encouraged to record when each of the three protocols will be implemented. This section also includes a space to record the outputs of those conversations. The second section provides a scheduler for one teaching and learning cycle. Here, facilitators can schedule each conversation, including classroom observations, and identify who will fulfill key roles. There is also space for simple notes. Finally, the third section focuses on Phase 3 and is organized similarly to the other sections. There is no section for Phase 4, as this is a schoolwide event.

PLC SCHEDULING TOOL

PLC:
Facilitator:

Phase 1: Preparing for Teaching and Learning Cycles

Meeting	Date	Details
Establish Team Norms		Key Roles Recorder: Timekeeper:

Notes: Final Norms

Set Student Learning Goals		Key Roles Recorder: Timekeeper:

Notes: Student Learning Goal

Set Teaching Improvement Goals		Key Roles Recorder: Timekeeper:

Notes: Teaching Improvement Goal

Phase 2: Engaging in Teaching and Learning Cycles (Cycle #:)

Meeting	Date	Details	Notes
Analyzing Standards		Roles Presenter: Recorder: Timekeeper:	
Lesson Tuning		Roles Presenter: Recorder: Timekeeper:	
Classroom Observation		Key Roles Teacher: Observers:	

Meeting	Date	Details	Notes
Observation Discussion		Observed Teacher: Recorder: Timekeeper:	
Analysis of Student Work		Key Roles Teacher: Recorder: Timekeeper:	

Phase 3: Studying the Impact on Student Learning and Teacher Practice

Meeting	Date	Details
Monitor Progress of Learning		Roles Recorder: Timekeeper:

Notes

START A FACILITATOR PLC

One final recommendation for new VITAL facilitators is to develop a Facilitator PLC dedicated to VITAL Collaboration. Such a PLC can be an excellent space for facilitators to practice using VITAL protocols for the first time, allowing them to gain confidence before implementing them with their teams. In the *School Leader's Guide to VITAL Collaboration*, we recommend that school leaders establish this type of PLC for teacher leaders. Facilitators in this group can also benefit from reading the chapters in Part II of this book together, fostering a deeper understanding of VITAL Collaboration. Another effective strategy is for members of a Facilitator PLC to role-play challenging situations that might arise during their work, helping them prepare for and navigate these situations successfully.

CONCLUSION

Getting started with VITAL Collaboration involves careful preparation and a commitment to continuous learning and improvement. By using the tools and strategies suggested in this chapter, such as developing a structured meeting schedule, engaging in reflective practices, and establishing a Facilitator PLC, facilitators can create a strong foundation for the type of productive collaboration that VITAL Collaboration fosters. Remember, building effective collaboration takes time and requires consistent effort, reflection, and adaptation. With these supports in place, facilitators will be better prepared to guide their PLCs through the four phases of VITAL Collaboration, leading to improvements in teaching practices and ultimately greater student learning outcomes.

CHAPTER 18

Crafting SMART Goals for PLCs

INTRODUCTION

Within Professional Learning Communities (PLCs), goal-setting is essential for guiding collaborative efforts and fostering continuous improvement in teaching and learning. One of the most effective tools for PLCs to use in this process is the SMART goal framework. SMART goals—Specific, Measurable, Achievable, Relevant, and Time-bound—provide a clear, structured approach to setting objectives that are actionable and aligned with both individual teacher development and broader schoolwide initiatives. By adopting SMART goals, PLCs can ensure that their collaborative work is focused, data-driven, and designed to yield tangible improvements in both teaching practices and student outcomes. This chapter explores how PLCs can effectively use SMART goals to enhance their collective efforts, overcome common challenges, and sustain continuous growth.

DEFINITION

SMART goals have become a widely adopted framework in education due to their ability to drive focused, results-oriented improvement in instructional practices and student outcomes. The SMART acronym (Specific, Measurable, Achievable, Relevant, and Time-bound) can be traced back to Doran (1981) and has since been refined and expanded through research across various fields, including education. More recent studies, such as that of Locke and Latham (2019), emphasize the importance of clear, well-defined goals in enhancing individual and group performance. In the context of Professional Learning Communities (PLCs), the use of SMART goals allows educators to set clear objectives that are aligned with both student needs and school improvement strategies. Below is a brief description of each characteristic in the acronym.

- **Specific:** According to research by Grant (2020), specific goals increase the likelihood of success by clarifying the exact outcome that is being pursued. In PLCs, specificity ensures that the team has a shared understanding of what they are working to achieve, which is crucial for collaborative efforts.

- **Measurable:** A study by Reeves (2004) highlights the significance of measurable goals in promoting accountability and progress tracking. Measurability allows PLCs to assess their performance over time and make data-driven adjustments to improve teaching and learning.
- **Achievable:** The importance of setting realistic and attainable goals is supported by research from Mager and Clark (2018), who found that goals perceived as achievable lead to greater motivation and persistence among team members. In PLCs, achievable goals ensure that teams are not overwhelmed and can make steady progress.
- **Relevant:** Relevance is a critical aspect of goal-setting, as goals must align with broader educational priorities. A study by Fullan (2021) shows that relevant goals help educators stay focused on meaningful improvements that are tied to student learning outcomes. For PLCs, this means that goals should directly address instructional needs and be linked to the overall mission of the school or district.
- **Time-bound:** Research by Moran and Torgeson (2017) underscores the importance of deadlines in goal achievement. Time-bound goals provide a sense of urgency and help PLCs maintain momentum by establishing clear timelines for reviewing progress and achieving outcomes.

In sum, the SMART goal framework can help PLCs can craft goals that not only set clear directions, but which also ensure that the goals are realistic, trackable, and aligned with student, teacher, and school needs.

GUIDANCE FOR CRAFTING SMART GOALS

Writing SMART goals is not just about following a protocol; it requires an understanding of how to translate data and observations into actionable and meaningful objectives. Below is some guidance to assist PLCs working on crafting SMART goals to enhance teaching and learning, particularly teams striving to develop student learning goals and goals to improve teaching practice.

Begin With Data Reflection

The foundation of any SMART goal should be a careful analysis of data. This could include student assessment results, classroom observation notes, or even feedback from previous PLC discussions. Rather than immediately jumping to solutions, PLC members should first reflect on what the data reveals about student learning and instructional practices. The goal-setting process will be more focused and relevant when grounded in an authentic understanding of current challenges. For example, a PLC might notice that students in a particular grade level are consistently underperforming in math problem-solving, and this could become the focus area for improvement.

Ensure Collective Input

While one person may take the lead in drafting a SMART goal, it is crucial that the entire PLC is involved in shaping the objective. Each member brings a unique perspective, and including input from the group ensures that the goal reflects the collective priorities of the team. Collaborative input also enhances commitment to the goal. Without this shared investment, even well-crafted goals can fail to generate momentum.

Clarify the Specifics

One of the key features of SMART goals is that they must be specific. A common pitfall in goal-setting is making objectives too broad or general, which can leave the PLC without clear direction. For instance, instead of setting a goal like "improve student engagement," it would be more effective to specify what aspect of engagement the team will focus on, such as "increase student participation during guided reading by incorporating structured questioning techniques." The more detailed and explicit the goal, the easier it will be for the PLC to align its efforts and measure progress.

Define Measurable Indicators of Success

Once a goal is set, the PLC must determine how they will measure success. This could involve quantitative data, such as test scores or assignment completion rates, or qualitative data, like student reflections or classroom observation notes. The key is to ensure that these indicators are directly tied to the goal. A measurable outcome for a reading engagement goal, for example, might be, "80% of students will participate at least three times during guided reading sessions by the end of the quarter." Defining such metrics upfront will help the team track progress more effectively.

Assess Feasibility

Goals must be realistic and achievable. In some cases, a PLC might be enthusiastic about a goal but may need to scale back the scope to make it attainable. It's essential to consider factors like time, resources, and support when determining the achievability of a goal. For example, a goal to raise all students' reading levels by two grades within a semester may not be feasible, but a goal to have 70% of students improve by one grade level could be. Feasibility ensures that PLC members feel empowered rather than discouraged as they work toward the goal.

Align With Broader School Priorities

Relevance is critical to ensuring that SMART goals contribute meaningfully to both the PLC's work and the overall goals of the school. Each goal should connect directly to broader initiatives or school improvement plans. For example, if a school's priority is improving literacy across grade levels, the PLC's goals should tie into that initiative. This alignment ensures that the PLC's efforts are not isolated but are part of a larger movement toward schoolwide improvement.

Establish a Realistic Timeline

Time-bound goals prevent work from drifting indefinitely. However, timelines should be flexible enough to accommodate the natural ebb and flow of teaching. A PLC might set a goal for the semester with key check-in points along the way. For example, a timeline could be, "By the end of the first quarter, 75% of students will meet the criteria for proficient problem-solving in math, with a midpoint review after 6 weeks." Timelines help keep the PLC focused and provide opportunities to adjust strategies as needed.

Examples of SMART Goals

To illustrate how SMART goals can be applied in different educational contexts, below are examples at the elementary, middle, and high school level.

Elementary Example 1

- Specific Goal: Increase the percentage of students reading at or above grade level by using guided reading sessions three times a week.
- SMART Goal: By the end of the school year, 90% of students will demonstrate reading proficiency as measured by the district reading benchmark assessment.

Elementary Example 2

- Specific Goal: Improve student phonemic awareness by incorporating daily phonics drills for 10 minutes each morning.

- SMART Goal: By the end of the semester, 85% of students will demonstrate mastery of grade-level phonemic awareness as measured by the quarterly literacy assessment.

Middle School Example 1

- Specific Goal: Improve student engagement and performance in math by implementing differentiated instruction during problem-solving activities.
- SMART Goal: By the end of the semester, 80% of students will achieve a passing score on the math unit assessments.

Middle School Example 2:

- Specific Goal: Increase student participation in collaborative learning by incorporating structured group activities twice a week in science.
- SMART Goal: By the end of the term, 75% of students will actively participate in group discussions and activities as measured by teacher observation and participation logs.

High School Example 1

- Specific Goal: Enhance critical thinking skills in social studies by incorporating primary source analysis in weekly lessons.
- SMART Goal: By the end of the semester, 85% of students will score at least a 4 on the critical thinking rubric.

High School Example 2

- Specific Goal: Improve student writing proficiency by implementing a peer review process for essay drafts in English.
- SMART Goal: By the end of the semester, 80% of students will improve their writing scores by one level on the district rubric after engaging in peer review.

Common Challenges With Writing SMART Goals

Despite the benefits of using SMART goals, there are common challenges that PLCs may face in the goal-setting process. Below are some typical obstacles and strategies to overcome them:

Overly Ambitious Goals. PLCs may set goals that are too ambitious given the available time and resources. It's important to balance ambition with achievability. Focus on smaller, more incremental goals that can build toward larger objectives.

Vague or Unclear Language. When goals are not specific enough, it can be difficult to determine what success looks like. PLCs should aim for clear, precise language when crafting their goals. This ensures that all members of the team have a shared understanding of what they are working toward.

Lack of Alignment With School Goals. Goals that are not aligned with the overall mission of the school can lead to disjointed efforts. It is essential to regularly check that SMART goals are tied to broader school or district priorities, ensuring that the PLC's work contributes to meaningful improvements in teaching and learning.

Insufficient Time Boundaries. Without clear deadlines, goals may lose their sense of urgency. PLCs should establish realistic timelines that create a sense of forward momentum, while also providing enough flexibility to accommodate unexpected challenges.

CONCLUSION

SMART goals provide PLCs with a powerful framework for setting objectives that drive meaningful improvements in both teaching practices and student learning outcomes. By following the SMART framework—ensuring goals are Specific, Measurable, Achievable, Relevant, and Time-bound—PLCs can create focused, actionable plans that lead to sustained professional growth. As PLCs continue to refine their goal-setting practices, they will be better equipped to overcome common challenges, align their efforts with broader school priorities, and ultimately foster a culture of continuous improvement.

CHAPTER 19

Why Standards Are Difficult to Understand

INTRODUCTION

Standards serve as the backbone for high-quality curriculum, instruction, and assessment, guiding what students should know and be able to do at each grade level, what teachers must teach, as well as what ultimately should get assessed. However, many educators find standards challenging to interpret and apply consistently in their classrooms. This chapter explores these challenges and emphasizes the need for routine collaborative analysis of standards in PLCs to develop a shared understanding of standards. It also highlights research that underscores the importance of standards and the necessity of analyzing and discussing them regularly.

THE IMPORTANCE OF STANDARDS AND REGULAR ANALYSIS

A range of research highlights the importance of standards in creating a consistent and equitable learning experience for all students. By setting clear expectations for learning, standards provide the foundation of a curriculum and help align instruction and assessment. Stormaiuolo and colleagues (2023) found that standards-based instruction positively impacts student achievement, particularly when educators use standards to guide lesson planning and to align teaching strategies, materials, and assessments. Similarly, Porter and colleagues (2011) emphasize that understanding the specific demands of standards is crucial for implementing standards-based instruction effectively in classrooms.

However, just having standards in place and embedded within high-quality curriculum materials is not enough. Teachers must also regularly "unpack" or analyze standards to apply them effectively in the classroom. Hord (1997) argues that when educators routinely collaborate to unpack and understand their standards, they strengthen collective efficacy and coherence in their instructional practices. Such routine analysis helps teachers identify what students need to learn, the depth of understanding required, and how best to assess mastery. Without regular discussions about the standards that are driving teaching and learning, teachers may interpret standards in isolation, leading to fragmented instructional practices that hinder student success. Thus, regular analysis of standards within PLCs is essential for achieving instructional alignment and ensuring high-quality education for all students.

WHY STANDARDS ARE DIFFICULT TO UNDERSTAND

Standards can be inherently difficult for educators to interpret and apply. The language used in standards often leaves room for multiple interpretations that can result in inconsistent implementation across classrooms and schools. Below are common ways standards present challenges, along with examples from various content areas and grade levels to illustrate these difficulties.

Ambiguity in Knowledge Demands

One common issue with standards is the ambiguity around the specific knowledge students need to acquire. For example, consider this 6th-grade English Language Arts standard from the Common Core: "Determine the meaning of words and phrases as they are used in a text, including figurative and connotative meanings; analyze the impact of a specific word choice on meaning and tone" (Common Core State Standards Initiative, 2010, ELA RL. 6.4). This standard identifies some of the big ideas and concepts students need to learn, such as figurative language, connotative language, meaning, and tone. At the same time, there is much that is implied and left ambiguous. For example, what types of figurative language are students expected to master? Should they explore metaphors, similes, irony, or allusions? Synecdoche or metonymy? Without further clarification, teachers are left to decide independently, which can lead to inconsistent instruction across classrooms.

A similar issue arises in mathematics. For instance, the Common Core Algebra standard on "Reasoning with Equations and Inequalities" requires students to "Understand solving equations as a process of reasoning and explain the reasoning" (Common Core State Standards Initiative, 2010, Math A-REI). The ambiguity here lies in how deeply students are expected to engage with this reasoning process. Are they simply explaining the procedures for each step (i.e., procedural knowledge), or do they need to know how to construct viable arguments and justify their methods? Such lack of specificity can result in varying levels of rigor and understanding.

Another layer of complexity and challenge related to knowledge in standards is imposed by the type of knowledge intended (declarative, procedural, or conditional) often being implied rather than stated. *Declarative knowledge* refers to the "what" of learning, encompassing facts and information that can be recalled and stated. Such knowledge is foundational to skills. *Procedural knowledge* involves understanding the "how," focusing on the steps and procedures for applying knowledge to solve problems. Procedural knowledge is a precursor to being able to competently demonstrate skills. *Conditional knowledge* is the highest level, involving an understanding of "when" and "why" to apply various types of knowledge in different contexts. Conditional knowledge requires knowing what information and skills to apply and how to adjust them across different situations and contexts. Together, these knowledge types form a continuum of metacognitive development, which can be bridged through adaptive interventions in learning environments (Abdelshiheed et al., 2023). The type of knowledge students are expected to master within a standards is often not stated; rather, it is almost always implied. Thus, teachers need to analyze the standards together to come to a common consensus on the type of knowledge students need to master with each standard.

Ambiguity in Skill Demands

Skill demands in standards can also be unclear. For example, a 2nd-grade social studies standard might state: "Recognize different forms of evidence used to make meaning in social studies (including primary and secondary sources, such as art, photographs, artifacts, oral histories, maps, and graphs)" (New York State Education Department, 2014, Grade 2 Social Studies Framework). The verb "recognize" is problematic because it implies an internal cognitive process without indicating how students should demonstrate this recognition. One teacher might interpret this standard as requiring students to identify whether a resource is a primary or secondary source, while another might teach and expect students to explain why certain forms of evidence are useful for understanding historical events. Another teacher might ask students to create or produce their own examples of maps and oral histories.

Similarly, in science, a middle school standard might require students to "analyze data to provide evidence for the effects of resource availability on organisms and populations of organisms in an ecosystem" (NGSS Lead States, 2013, MS-LS2-1). The term "analyze" in this standard can also lead to various interpretations. Does it mean creating data tables, interpreting graphs, or drawing conclusions based on evidence? Without clear guidelines, teachers might approach this standard differently, leading to inconsistencies in instruction and ultimately variance in student learning experiences.

Ambiguity in Rigor Demands

Building on the previous two challenges, another difficulty is understanding the level of rigor that a standard intends or requires. For instance, the high school Algebra standard mentioned earlier not only requires students to "explain their process for solving a problem" but also to "construct a viable argument to justify their approach." Teachers might overlook the compound nature of this standard, focusing solely on the procedural aspect (explaining how they solved it) rather than the conceptual understanding (justifying why their method is correct). This can lead to instruction that lacks the depth intended by the standard, causing gaps in students' mastery of key concepts.

In the English Language Arts standards, the Grade 7 version of the figurative language standard might require students to "analyze the impact of rhymes and other repetitions of sounds (e.g., alliteration) on a specific verse or stanza of a poem or section of a story or drama." This standard increases the rigor by introducing additional elements (such as rhymes and sound repetitions), but the degree to which students should analyze these features remains vague. Should they simply identify these elements, or do they need to explore how they shape meaning and tone within the text? Or, are they expected to reproduce these devices in their own writing? These nuances in rigor can significantly impact how teachers approach instruction.

The Added Complexity of English Language Development Standards

An additional layer of complexity arises when teachers integrate English Language Development (ELD) standards into their instruction alongside content standards. ELD standards are designed to support English learners (ELs) in acquiring both academic language and content knowledge. For example, the California ELD Standards for grades 6–8 require students to "Express ideas and opinions in increasingly detailed and complex ways" (California Department of Education, 2012, Part I: Section 3). Teachers often strive to weave this standard into their lesson plans while also addressing grade-level content standards. This integration requires careful scaffolding to support ELs in expressing their ideas using complex language while simultaneously grasping subject-specific content. The dual focus of addressing both language development and content mastery adds to the already intricate process of unpacking standards, requiring thoughtful planning and differentiation. Thus, aligning content standards with ELD standards heightens the need for regular analysis and collaboration within PLCs to ensure coherent and accessible instruction for all students.

THE IMPORTANCE OF ANALYZING STANDARDS COLLABORATIVELY

Given the complexities just described, routine analysis of standards in a collaborative setting is essential. PLCs provide the perfect environment for educators to collectively interpret standards, discuss their implications for instruction, and align their teaching practices. Analyzing a standard requires a multistep process that requires careful consideration and collaboration among teachers. To ensure consistency in interpretation and implementation, this process should be approached thoughtfully and methodically. The *Protocol for Analyzing Standards* described earlier in this book provides a structured approach for educators to navigate this complexity, and readers are encouraged to refer to it for a detailed guide.

The process for analyzing a standard process begins with teachers reading the standard closely, often multiple times, to familiarize themselves with the language and identify key terms, skills, and concepts. During this initial step, it's crucial for teachers to break the standard into its components, discussing what students need to know and be able to do. By examining the wording, educators can start to clarify the knowledge and skill demands that the standard implies.

After this close reading, the next step is to explore the standard's requirements in more depth. Teachers work together to define the specific knowledge and skills required, considering the rigor or depth of understanding that students must achieve. This phase often includes discussions around potential areas of misinterpretation, as standards can sometimes be vague or open to multiple interpretations. By engaging in this dialogue, teachers can reach a shared understanding of what the standard entails and how to teach it effectively.

Once they have clarified the knowledge and skills, educators collaboratively decide what evidence will indicate that students have met the standard. This involves selecting or designing assessments, student work products, or observable behaviors that align with the standard's expectations. Identifying these criteria is essential for ensuring that instruction and assessment are aligned and that students are meeting the intended learning goals.

This process, when undertaken routinely within PLCs, supports instructional coherence and helps educators develop a collective understanding of the standards. By following the *Protocol* for *Analyzing Standards* as a guide, teachers can ensure that their lessons are aligned with standards, thereby enhancing student learning experiences.

THE IMPORTANCE OF ANALYZING STANDARDS WITHIN THE CONTEXT OF INSTRUCTION

Finally, it is important to mention that it is ideal to analyze standards in the context of upcoming instruction, as this helps teachers design and refine their lessons effectively. On occasion we have seen schools and grade-level teams engage in large workshops where educators unpack all of the standards in their content area or grade level, standard by standard. We believe this is an inefficient use of time, because the unpacking is too distant from when teachers will actually teach each standard. By reviewing the standards that are most relevant to what students will be learning in the near future, educators can tailor their instruction to meet the specific expectations set forth in the standards. Thus, PLCS are an excellent place to do this as part of a teaching and learning cycle.

Similarly, when teachers have English learners in their classroom it is also important to analyze both the content and ELD standards for an upcoming lesson to ensure alignment. This dual analysis allows teachers to address language development while meeting content-specific learning goals, ensuring that all students receive the support they need. Through this ongoing, context-specific analysis within PLCs, teachers can enhance their instructional strategies, make informed decisions about the depth of knowledge required, and align their teaching practices to promote student mastery of the standards.

CONCLUSION

Standards are complex, and without routine collaboration, their ambiguity can lead to inconsistent teaching and learning. By regularly unpacking standards during PLC meetings in advance of upcoming instruction, educators can clarify their expectations, align their instructional practices, and ensure that all students receive a high-quality education. Incorporating routine standards analysis into PLCs is not just beneficial, it is essential. Without this process, teachers may continue to interpret standards in isolation, leading to fragmentation in curriculum and instruction. By fostering a culture of collaboration around standards, schools can ensure consistency and coherence, ultimately leading to greater student success.

Conclusion

REFLECTING ON THE JOURNEY OF VITAL COLLABORATION

As we come to the end of this journey, let us reflect on the purpose and intended impact of VITAL Collaboration. Throughout this book, we've explored the core principles and practices that make Professional Learning Communities (PLCs) a powerful tool for enhancing teaching and learning. The VITAL framework was designed to help you foster deep, meaningful collaboration that leads to positive changes in instructional practice and student outcomes. By embracing the steps laid out in this guide, you have taken strides toward building a culture of sustained professional growth.

THE ROLE OF TEACHERS AND TEACHER LEADERS

Teachers, whether they be facilitators or PLC members, are at the heart of VITAL Collaboration. Your role is essential in shaping how your PLCs function, engaging in the work with your colleagues, and ensuring that collaboration is effective and impactful. Throughout this book, we have highlighted the skills, tools, and strategies necessary for you to lead and participate with confidence, from creating clear agendas to using protocols that support structured, focused dialogue. By actively embracing the type of collaboration VITAL is designed to foster, you become a catalyst for positive change, helping your team and school build strong, effective collaborative practices that will have a positive and lasting impact on teaching and learning.

KEY ELEMENTS OF VITAL COLLABORATION: A RECAP

As you know by now, the VITAL Collaboration framework is built around four interconnected phases grounded in improvement science. Each phase contributes to the overall effectiveness of your PLC, and together they create a cycle of continuous improvement. The preparation phase lays the foundation by establishing roles, norms, and goals. The TLC phase focuses on deep conversations around instructional practice, using protocols to ensure productive discussions. The monitoring phase encourages teams to assess their progress and learn from their experiences, while the share and celebrate phase engages the entire school community in learning and growing together. By integrating these phases, VITAL Collaboration provides a structured yet flexible approach that adapts drives ongoing improvement.

IMPACT ON TEACHING PRACTICES AND STUDENT LEARNING

At its core, VITAL Collaboration is about improving teaching practices to enhance student learning. The strategies and protocols shared throughout this book are not just theoretical, they are practical tools that have been field-tested in real schools and can be applied directly to your work. When facilitators and PLC members commit to thoughtful collaboration, the impact is felt not only in improved teaching practices but also in student outcomes. For example, when a PLC effectively uses the *Protocol for Analyzing Student Work*, teachers gain deeper insights into how their instructional choices affect student learning, allowing them to make informed adjustments that directly benefit students.

SUSTAINING AND SCALING VITAL COLLABORATION

The journey of VITAL Collaboration does not end with the final page of this book. Sustaining the momentum of VITAL Collaboration requires ongoing commitment and reflection. Revisit the protocols, assess the effectiveness of your PLCs, and adjust as needed. Growth is an iterative process, and by continually reflecting on your practices, you can keep your PLCs moving forward. Moreover, the impact of VITAL Collaboration can be expanded beyond individual PLCs. When we share successes and challenges across teams and schools, the principles of VITAL Collaboration can take root at a broader scale, fostering a culture of continuous learning across your entire school or district.

THE FUTURE OF PROFESSIONAL LEARNING AND COLLABORATION

Looking ahead, the future of professional learning will continue to be shaped by collaboration. In an ever-changing educational landscape, the ability to work together, share insights, and adapt is more important than ever. VITAL Collaboration provides a framework that not only enhances individual teacher practice but also strengthens the collective capacity of schools to navigate new challenges. The need for adaptability, reflection, and a commitment to growth will continue to be at the heart of effective professional learning. By embracing VITAL Collaboration, you are positioning yourself and your school to meet these future challenges head-on.

FINAL THOUGHTS AND CALL TO ACTION

As we conclude, we want to leave you with an inspirational message: The power of VITAL Collaboration lies in the *collective* commitment to growth, learning, and student success. Facilitators, teacher leaders, and school leaders all have a role to play in fostering a collaborative culture that drives improvement. Take what you have learned from this book and apply it to your unique context. Use the tools, strategies, and protocols to bring about meaningful change. Be an agent of change in your school, lead your PLCs with purpose, and inspire your colleagues to do the same. Together, through VITAL Collaboration, we can create schools where every educator and every student has the opportunity to thrive.

References

Abdelshiheed, M., Hostetter, J. W., Barnes, T., & Chi, M. (2023). *Bridging declarative, procedural, and conditional metacognitive knowledge gap using deep reinforcement learning*. CogSci '23, The 45th International Conference of the Cognitive Science Society (Sydney, Australia). https://www.researchgate.net/publication/370926538_Bridging_Declarative_Procedural_and_Conditional_Metacognitive_Knowledge_Gap_Using_Deep_Reinforcement_Learning

Bandura, A. (1997). *Self-efficacy: The exercise of control*. Freeman.

Berry, A. (2022). *Reimagining student engagement: From disrupting to driving*. Corwin Press.

Bryk, A. S., Gomez, L. M., & Grunow, A. (2011). Getting ideas into action: Building networked improvement communities in education. In M. E. Hallinan (Ed.), *Frontiers in sociology of education* (pp. 127–162). Springer Netherlands.

Bushe, G. R. (2012). Appreciative inquiry: Theory and critique. In D. Boje, B. Burnes, & J. Hassard (Eds.), *The Routledge companion to organizational change* (pp. 87–103). Routledge.

California Department of Education. (2012). *California English language development standards: Kindergarten through grade 12*. https://www.cde.ca.gov/sp/el/er/eldstandards.asp

Carmi, T., Guberman, A., & Cohen Brandeis, R. (2022). PLC tools: Promoting learning about learning in a teachers' professional community. *Professional Development in Education*, 1–16.

Collin, J., & Smith, E. (2021). *Effective professional development* [*Guidance report]*. Education Endowment Foundation.

Common Core State Standards Initiative. (2010). *Common Core state standards for English Language Arts & Literacy in History/Social Studies, Science, and technical subjects*. http://www.thecorestandards.org/ELA-Literacy/

Common Core State Standards Initiative. (2010). *Common Core state standards for mathematics*. http://www.corestandards.org/Math/

Cooperrider, D. L., Stavros, J. M., & Whitney, D. (2008). *The appreciative inquiry handbook: For leaders of change* (2nd ed.) Berrett-Koehler Publishers.

Covey, S. R. (2020). *The 7 habits of highly effective people*. Simon & Schuster.

Dalessio, S. J. (2019). A tutorial for implementing strategic questioning in the clinical teaching environment. *Perspectives of the ASHA Special Interest Groups, 4*(6), 1465–1472.

Darling-Hammond, L., Hyler, M. E., & Gardner, M. (2017). *Effective teacher professional development*. Learning Policy Institute.

De Jong, L., Meirink, J., & Admiraal, W. (2022). School-based collaboration as a learning context for teachers: A systematic review. *International Journal of Educational Research, 112*, 101927.

Desimone, L. M., & Garet, M. S. (2015). Best practices in teachers' professional development in the United States. *Psychology, Society, and Education, 7*(3), 252–263.

Dogan, S., Yurtseven, N., & Tatık, R. Ş. (2019). Meeting agenda matters: Promoting reflective dialogue in teacher communities. *Professional Development in Education, 45*(2), 231–249.

Donohoo, J., Hattie, J., & Eells, R. (2018). The power of collective efficacy. *Educational Leadership, 75*(6), 40–44.

Doran, G. T. (1981). There's a SMART way to write management's goals and objectives. *Management Review, 70*(11), 35–36.

Douglas, T. (2024). *A qualitative study examining perceptions of effectiveness of PLCs for building collective teacher efficacy* (Publication No. 31239111) [Doctoral dissertation, Evangel University]. ProQuest Dissertations & Theses. https://www.proquest.com/docview/3051835840

DuFour, R., & Eaker, R. (1998). *Professional learning communities at work: Best practices for enhancing student achievement*. National Educational Service.

Edmondson, A. C., & Bransby, D. P. (2023). Psychological safety comes of age: Observed themes in an established literature. *Annual Review of Organizational Psychology and Organizational Behavior, 10*(1), 55–78.

Follmer, D. J., Groth, R., Bergner, J., & Weaver, S. (2024). Theory-based evaluation of lesson study professional development: Challenges, opportunities, and lessons learned. *American Journal of Evaluation, 45*(2), 292–312.

Forsythe, A., & Johnson, S. (2017). Thanks, but no-thanks for the feedback. *Assessment & Evaluation in Higher Education, 42*(6), 850–859.

Fullan, M. (2021). *Leading in a culture of change*. Jossey-Bass.

Garmston, R. J., & Wellman, B. M. (2016). *The adaptive school: A sourcebook for developing collaborative groups*. Rowman & Littlefield.

Goddard, R. D., Hoy, W. K., & Hoy, A. W. (2004). Collective efficacy beliefs: Theoretical developments, empirical evidence, and future directions. *Educational Researcher, 33*(3), 3–13.

Goddard, R. D., Skrla, L., & Salloum, S. J. (2017). The role of collective efficacy in closing student achievement gaps: A mixed methods study of school leadership for excellence and equity. *Journal of Education for Students Placed at Risk, 22*(1), 1–17.

Grant, A. M. (2020). *The effectiveness of SMART goals in professional development*. Routledge.

Harris, A., & Jones, M. (2010). Professional learning communities and system improvement. *Improving Schools, 13*(2), 172–181.

Hattie, J. (2009). *Visible learning: A synthesis of over 800 meta-analyses relating to achievement*. Routledge.

Hattie, J. (2023). *Visible learning: The sequel: A synthesis of over 2,100 meta-analyses relating to achievement*. Routledge.

Hattie, J., & Timperley, H. (2007). The power of feedback. *Review of Educational Research, 77*(1), 81–112.

Hattie, J., & Zierer, K. (2019). *Visible learning insights*. Routledge.

Hoogsteen, T. J. (2020). Collective efficacy: Toward a new narrative of its development and role in achievement. *Palgrave Communications, 6*(1), 1–7.

Hord, S. M. (1997). *Professional learning communities: Communities of continuous inquiry and improvement*. Southwest Educational Development Laboratory.

Hord, S. M., Abrego, J., Moller, G., Olivier, D. F., Pankake, A. M., & Roundtree, L. (2010). *Demystifying professional learning communities: School leadership at its best*. Rowman & Littlefield Education.

Institute for Healthcare Improvement Multimedia Team. (2015). *Like magic? ("Every system is perfectly designed . . .")*. Institute for Healthcare Improvement. https://www.ihi.org/insights/magic-every-system-perfectly-designed

Jay, J. K., & Johnson, K. L. (2002). Capturing complexity: A typology of reflective practice for teacher education. *Teaching and teacher education, 18*(1), 73–85.

Johnson, S. (2010). *Where good ideas come from: The natural history of innovation*. Riverhead Books.

Kennedy, M. M. (2016). How does professional development improve teaching? *Review of Educational Research, 86*(4), 945–980.

Kluger, A. N., & DeNisi, A. (1996). The effects of feedback interventions on performance: A historical review, a meta-analysis, and a preliminary feedback intervention theory. *Psychological Bulletin, 119*(2), 254–284.

Lee, M., Kim, J. W., Mo, Y., & Walker, A. D. (2024). A review of professional learning community (PLC) instruments. *Journal of Educational Administration, 60*(3), 262–287.

Leithwood, K., Seashore, K., Anderson, S., & Wahlstrom, K. (2004). *Review of research: How leadership influences student learning*. University of Minnesota, Center for Applied Research and Educational Improvement.

LeMahieu, P. G., Edwards, A. R., & Gomez, L. M. (2015). At the nexus of improvement science and teaching: Introduction to a special section of the *Journal of Teacher Education, 66*(5), 446–449.

LeMahieu, P. G., Grunow, A., Baker, L., Nordstrum, L. E., & Gomez, L. M. (2017). Networked improvement communities: The discipline of improvement science meets the power of networks. *Quality Assurance in Education, 25*(1), 5–25.

Lewis, C. (2015). What is improvement science? Do we need it in education? *Educational Researcher, 44*(1), 54–61.

Linder, R. A., Post, G., & Calabrese, K. (2012). Professional learning communities: Practices for successful implementation. *Delta Kappa Gamma Bulletin, 78*(3), 13–22.

Locke, E. A., & Latham, G. P. (2019). Building a practically useful theory of goal setting and task motivation. *American Psychologist, 57*(9), 705–717.

Mager, R. F., & Clark, R. C. (2018). *Goal analysis: How to clarify your goals so you can actually achieve them*. Center for Effective Performance.

McKnight, L., & Whitburn, B. (2020). Seven reasons to question the hegemony of Visible Learning. *Discourse: Studies in the Cultural Politics of Education, 41*(1), 32–44.

McLaughlin, M. W., & Talbert, J. E. (2006). *Building school-based teacher learning communities: Professional strategies to improve student achievement*. Teachers College Press.

Moosa, V., Salleh, S., & Hamid, L. (2024). Defining and operationalizing professional learning communities: What does the literature say? *Asia Pacific Journal of Education, 44*(2), 475–487.

Moran, G., & Torgeson, C. J. (2017). The role of deadlines in goal achievement: A meta-analysis. *Journal of Educational Psychology, 109*(3), 467–483.

Mosoge, M. J., Challens, B. H., & Xaba, M. I. (2018). Perceived collective teacher efficacy in low performing schools. *South African Journal of Education, 38*(2), 1–9.

Murata, A. (2011). Introduction: Conceptual overview of lesson study. In L. C. Hart, A. S. Alston, & A. Murata (Eds.), *Lesson study research and practice in mathematics education: Learning together* (pp. 1–12). Springer.

National School Reform Faculty. (n.d.). *Text rendering experience protocol*. National School Reform Faculty Harmony Education Center. https://www.nsrfharmony.org/protocols/text-rendering-experience

New York State Education Department. (2014). *New York State K–8 Social Studies Framework*. https://www.engageny.org/resource/new-york-state-k-12-social-studies-framework

NGSS Lead States. 2013. *Next generation science standards: For states, by states*. The National Academies Press.

Nichols, M. P., & Straus, M. B. (2021). *The lost art of listening* (3rd ed.). Guilford Press.

Nielsen, K., & Klitmøller, J. (2021). Blind spots in visible learning: A critique of John Hattie as an educational theorist. *Nordic Psychology, 73*(3), 268–283

Nieto, S. (2015). *The light in their eyes: Creating multicultural learning communities*. Teachers College Press.

Popova, A., Evans, D. K., Breeding, M. E., & Arancibia, V. (2022). Teacher professional development around the world: The gap between evidence and practice. *The World Bank Research Observer, 37*(1), 107–136.

Porter, A., McMaken, J., Hwang, J., & Yang, R. (2011). Common Core standards: The new U.S. intended curriculum. *Educational Researcher, 40*(3), 103–116.

Reeves, D. B. (2004). *Accountability for learning: How teachers and school leaders can take charge*. ASCD.

Robinson, V. M., Lloyd, C. A., & Rowe, K. J. (2008). The impact of leadership on student outcomes: An analysis of the differential effects of leadership types. *Educational Administration Quarterly, 44*(5), 635–674.

Rømer, T. A. (2019). A critique of John Hattie's theory of Visible Learning. *Educational Philosophy and Theory, 51*(6), 587–598.

Ryan, R. M., & Deci, E. L. (2022). Self-determination theory. In *Encyclopedia of quality of life and well-being research* (pp. 1–7). Springer International Publishing.

Schön, D. A. (1994). *The reflective practitioner: How professionals think in action.* Routledge.

Sharrock, D., & Challen, C. (2023). Lesson study can build teachers' confidence in their practice. *The Learning Professional, 44*(5), 50–54.

Sims, S., & Fletcher-Wood, H. (2021). Identifying the characteristics of effective teacher professional development: A critical review. *School Effectiveness and School Improvement, 32*(1), 47–63.

Stoll, L., Bolam, R., McMahon, A., Wallace, M., & Thomas, S. (2006). Professional learning communities: A review of the literature. *Journal of Educational Change, 7*(4), 221–258.

Stone, D., & Heen, S. (2015). *Thanks for the feedback: The science and art of receiving feedback well.* Penguin.

Stone, D., Patton, B., & Heen, S. (2023). *Difficult conversations: How to discuss what matters most.* Penguin.

Stornaiuolo, A., Desimone, L., & Polikoff, M. (2023). "The good struggle" of flexible specificity: Districts balancing specific guidance with autonomy to support standards-based instruction. *American Educational Research Journal, 60*(3), 521–561.

van den Boom-Muilenburg, S. N., de Vries, S., van Veen, K., Poortman, C., & Schildkamp, K. (2022). Leadership practices and sustained lesson study. *Educational Research, 64*(3), 295–316.

Vescio, V., Ross, D., & Adams, A. (2008). A review of research on the impact of professional learning communities on teaching practice and student learning. *Teaching and Teacher Education, 24*(1), 80–91.

Voelkel, R. H., Jr., & Chrispeels, J. H. (2017). Understanding the link between professional learning communities and teacher collective efficacy. *School Effectiveness and School Improvement, 28*(4), 505–526.

Walsh, J. A., & Sattes, B. D. (2016). *Quality questioning: Research-based practice to engage every learner.* Corwin Press.

Watson, C. (2014). Effective professional learning communities? The possibilities for teachers as agents of change in schools. *British Educational Research Journal, 40*(1), 18–29.

Wisniewski, B., Zierer, K., & Hattie, J. (2020). The power of feedback revisited: A meta-analysis of educational feedback research. *Frontiers in Psychology, 10,* 487662.

Woodland, R. H. (2016). Evaluating PK–12 professional learning communities: An improvement science perspective. *American Journal of Evaluation, 37*(4), 505–521.

Wullschleger, A., Vörös, A., Rechsteiner, B., Rickenbacher, A., & Merki, K. M. (2023). Improving teaching, teamwork, and school organization: Collaboration networks in school teams. *Teaching and Teacher Education, 121,* 103909.

Index

About the Author

Kevin Perks is a senior director at WestEd, where he leads the development and implementation of school and district improvement services across the country. He works with schools, districts, and state education agencies, applying his expertise to direct a team of over 40 staff who provide a wide range of services in school improvement, leadership coaching, standards-aligned curriculum, instruction, assessment, literacy, as well as family and student engagement. His efforts are particularly focused on driving equitable school improvement for historically underserved students. Kevin is the editor of *Transformational Leadership for Rapid School Improvement* and the coauthor of *Motivation to Learn: Transforming Classroom Culture to Support Student Achievement*. Before joining WestEd, Kevin served as a district leader, school leader, instructional coach, and teacher at the elementary, middle, and high school levels.

About WestEd

As a national leader in research, development, and professional service, WestEd is reimagining solutions to a more equitable society by taking on the most demanding and enduring challenges in education and human development. As a nonpartisan agency, WestEd's mission is to work with education and other communities to promote excellence, achieve equity, and improve learning for children, youth, and adults. To achieve this mission, WestEd staff work collaboratively systemwide to provide a broad range of services, including research and evaluation, professional learning, technical assistance, and policy guidance, that are tailored to the needs of clients. As a nonpartisan partner, WestEd generates knowledge and applies evidence and expertise to improve policies, systems, and practices. A steadfast commitment to equity, diversity, and inclusion is central to WestEd's work to advance equitable opportunities, increase well-being, and promote positive outcomes for all children, youth, and adults. Visit Wested.org to learn more.